# Smoke Across the Fells

MICHAEL WELCH

Rails

Published by Rails Publishing

Printed by Parksons Graphics

© Michael Welch 2017
Layout by Michael Welch. Typesetting
and book production by Lucy Frontani.

*Front Cover:* BR Standard Class 9F 2-10-0
No.92051 climbs the final few yards to Ais
Gill summit with a Long Meg sidings to
Widnes mineral train. *Colour-Rail*

*Back cover:* Hardendale quarry lies just
north of Shap summit and in this portrait
BR Standard 'Clan' Pacific No.72007 *Clan
Mackintosh* is depicted shunting in the
sidings which give access to the quarry
while, in the background, an unidentified
BR Standard 2-10-0 with a Crosti-boiler
approaches on a southbound goods.
*The late Derek Cross*

*Title page:* Judging by the heavy frost on
the surrounding fields 31st January 1965
dawned bitterly cold in the Carlisle area but
such conditions are ideal for steam railway
photography, and here the photographer
has taken maximum advantage to produce
this stirring shot. Unfortunately, the identity
of the train is unknown, but at least the
locomotive's number is visible. It is Stanier
Class 5MT No.44692, complete with a
miniature snow plough, and this portrait
was taken just north of the former Cotehill
station. There was a station here, but the
small hamlet of Cotehill was more than
a mile distant and perhaps local people
preferred to use the bus service, the station
closing from 5th April 1952. The station
was demolished very soon after closure
and no trace now remains; however, the
stationmaster's house and row of four
cottages survive. *Bob Leslie/Peter Robinson
collection*

Details of Michael Welch's other
railway titles can be found at
www.capitaltransport.com

# Introduction

On the morning of 20th January 1962 two highly polished BR Standard 2-6-0s, Class 3MT No.77003 and Class 4MT No.76049, were no doubt the principal topic of conversation among the many railway enthusiasts gathered on Darlington station. But the sparkling condition of the two 'Moguls' could do little to lift the spirits of those present and the all-pervading mood was one of sadness and gloom because they were about to haul the final steam train over the outstanding route to Penrith and Tebay which climbed to a summit of 1,370 feet above sea level at Stainmore, the highest point on any line in England.

One of my everlasting regrets is the fact that I never travelled over this bleak but magnificent line across the north Pennines. What an incredible route that was, with challenging gradients of 1 in 59/60, lofty viaducts providing spectacular views and mile after mile of barren, inhospitable moorland as the route climbed to Stainmore summit. This line also boasted particularly interesting motive power in the shape of the BR Class 3MT 2-6-0 and 2-6-2T locomotives, two of the smaller BR Standard classes. Operationally, the Tebay to Kirkby Stephen East section, which closed to regular passenger trains in 1952, was one of those routes that made the study of railways so fascinating and rewarding. This moribund stretch remained open for goods traffic and came to life every summer when 'mystery' holiday trains from the north-east to Blackpool were routed that way, but were not advertised between Kirkby Stephen and Tebay. So, if a young lad on one of those services looked out of the window and asked his parents where they were they could be forgiven if they didn't know!

Another especially attractive line was the route from Penrith to Workington which passed through Keswick, a town that for many people is the 'capital' of the Lake District. Like the Stainmore line this route abounded with fierce gradients, also boasted some magnificent scenery and had a particularly beautiful section where the railway ran alongside the placid waters of Bassenthwaite Lake. This line never achieved a high profile among the steam enthusiast fraternity due to the introduction of diesel multiple units on most local trains as early as 1955 but steam traction in the shape of Ivatt Class 2MT 2-6-0s remained in control of the 'Lakes Express' and, in addition, larger motive power in the form of 'Royal Scots' and 'Jubilees' put in appearances on a regular summer excursion from Newcastle-upon-Tyne. The line was closed in stages, the section west of Keswick succumbing from 18th April 1966, while the remaining stub from Penrith survived for a further six years until that, too, was closed from 6th March 1972. The last steam working to traverse the entire route was a rail tour from Manchester on 2nd April 1966, a day when a blizzard engulfed the north of England so it was a day to remember in more ways than one.

The three branch lines with the highest profile in the area covered by this book are those to Coniston, Lake Side and Windermere and these lines have had very mixed fortunes. The branch from Foxfield to Coniston was remote from the major centres of population in the north of England and became a relatively early casualty, closing from 6th October 1958. The Lake Side branch has a complicated history because its regular passenger trains from Ulverston were withdrawn as long ago as 26th September 1938 but, apart from the duration of the Second World War, passenger workings continued during the summer until 6th September 1965. Following closure the line attracted the attention of preservationists who wished to operate a tourist railway and they no doubt recognised the branch's potential, bearing in mind the terminus was adjacent to a steamer terminal on Lake Windermere. Unfortunately, their plans were thwarted by a road scheme and the line was severed south of Haverthwaite, but at least the short section from Lake Side station has survived and continues to offer tourists a nostalgic, and quite scenic, run behind steam traction during the summer. Regrettably, the impressive station building at Lake Side was razed to the ground in the late 1970s, a sad loss to the preservation movement. The branch from Oxenholme to Windermere probably has the best service in its history, but the original station building at Windermere is now a supermarket and the former four platform layout was sacrificed as a result of over zealous 'rationalisation', leaving a very basic station which is a pale shadow of former, more prosperous years.

The West Coast Main Line (WCML) is probably busier today than it ever has been but the section from Carnforth to Carlisle has certainly lost its 'soul'. In steam days there was a seemingly endless procession of goods trains which normally needed banking assistance up to Grayrigg and Shap summits. There was the ritual of the train engine and 'banker' exchanging whistles before plodding up the gradient at walking pace and the sound echoed across the fells, so observers at Shap Wells, for example, usually had plenty of warning that something was coming, provided the wind was in the right direction. Today, the character of the line has changed beyond recognition. There are overhead wires, the signal boxes and most intermediate stations have gone, and the noisy and intrusive M6 motorway shares the Lune gorge with the railway while trains cruise up to Shap summit at almost top speed. The neighbouring Settle and Carlisle route has also undergone changes but to a much lesser degree and, despite the loss of originating traffic from locations such as Long Meg and the closure of signal boxes, the line still retains much of its original infrastructure; even most of the long-closed stations survive in some form. Needless to say, the weather is still as unpredictable and violent as ever, so nothing has changed there! Another route that maintains a distinctive atmosphere is that between Carnforth and Carlisle via Barrow-in-Furness. There are stretches that cross wide estuaries, skirt the Lake District, run alongside the sea and twist and turn beneath the cliffs near Whitehaven, so it is a route not without interest. Virtually untouched by modernisation, many stations and signal boxes survive intact but, regrettably, much of the area's heavy industry has long since disappeared and with it the fascinating network of lines that once served the coal and iron industries in west Cumberland.

Compilation of this album has benefited from assistance provided by Chris Evans, Dave Fakes, John Langford and Terry Phillips who suggested many amendments and improvements to the text. Pictures from the Armstrong Railway Photographic Trust were kindly made available by Richard Barber while those taken by the late Bob Leslie were provided by Peter Robinson. In addition, David Cross submitted photographs taken by his late father, Rodney Lissenden supplied those taken by David Clark while Bob Bridger made available Charles Firminger's pictures. Assistance was also provided by Ron Herbert. I am most grateful to all of these gentlemen for their kind support.

*Michael Welch*
*Burgess Hill*
*West Sussex*

# Contents

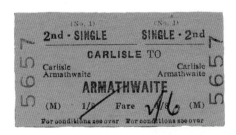

On 25th June 1840 the Lancaster and Preston Junction Railway opened, and Lancaster was brought within eleven hours of London. Initially there was no connection at Preston with the North Union Railway and passengers had to change, but that was a minor inconvenience compared to the rigours of stage coach travel. Thoughts now turned to a route to Scotland which had been one of the ultimate objectives of the Grand Junction Railway (GJR) since its inception. Joseph Locke and George Stephenson had visited the Carlisle area in 1835, the former surveying a route on behalf of the GJR, but opinions differed regarding the most practical route northwards. The mountains of the Lake District presented a formidable obstacle, and the idea of building a railway through such inhospitable terrain presented a daunting challenge but, even so, Locke considered various routes. In contrast Stephenson wished to avoid the fells altogether and proposed a barrage across Morecambe bay and a circuitous line along the Cumberland coast where it would join a projected extension of the Maryport and Carlisle Railway. A further complication was the involvement of Cornelius Nicholson, a prominent citizen of Kendal, who wished to see his town served by any new route to the north, and a local committee suggested a route from Kendal up Longsleddale, a deep valley surrounded by rugged mountains. A two miles-long tunnel would have been needed at the head of the valley before trains emerged on the shore of Haweswater; however this line, which would certainly have been spectacular, was not seriously considered. The government appointed a Royal Commission to examine the merits of all the various schemes and it came out decisively against the lengthy coastal route so, in February 1840, the members began a personal inspection of the inland routes that had been proposed. Plans were already being made for a line to Scotland over Beattock summit and with this in mind, and the challenge of the East Coast route in the background, in March 1842 Locke decided to submit two alternative routes to Parliament, one via Kirkby Lonsdale and the other through Oxenholme to appease Kendal folk; both threaded the Lune Valley. On 5th June 1844 the construction of the Lancaster to Carlisle line was approved by Parliament and received the Royal Assent the following day; the GJR subscribed much of the capital for the works. The first sod was cut near Birkbeck viaduct only a month later and the first permanent rail was laid on Shap fell on 18th November 1844. The man in charge of construction was Thomas Brassey, the legendary engineer who is reputed to have built one mile of railway out of every twenty constructed up to the time of his death. Locke opted to serve Kendal by taking the tracks through Oxenholme and, in order to reduce costs, decided to take the line over Shap Fell on a 1 in 75 gradient. By the end of 1844 3,761 men and 387 horses were employed and construction proceeded at a furious pace; one of the major obstacles was removal of 350,000 cubic yards of material to create a cutting just south of Shap summit.

The navvies often laboured in appalling conditions and tensions sometimes boiled over, but the brilliant organisation of Thomas Brassey ensured that progress continued unabated and on 5th November 1846 members of the Board of Trade carried out an inspection. The formal opening took place on 15th December and through passenger traffic from London to Scotland commenced on 15th February 1848 when the Caledonian Railway's line from Carlisle to Glasgow was brought into use. The East Coast line was largely complete by that date apart from two substantial bridges across the rivers Tyne and Tweed and it was a further two years before through trains started on the rival route. Here, Stanier Class 5MT 4-6-0 No.45131 is seen leaving Carnforth with a rake of empty wagons in tow on 22nd May 1964. *Noel Machell*

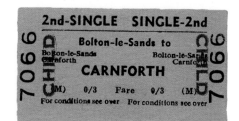

*THE WEST COAST MAIN LINE*

Three pre-grouping companies had sheds at Carnforth and all of these lasted well into the 1930s. In 1938 the LMSR announced a modernisation plan for the station and this included a new locomotive depot to be erected on the site of the Furness Railway (FR) building. The new shed was to be equipped with mechanical coaling and ash disposal facilities, a 70ft turntable, 75,000-gallon water tank and a modern repair shop. The turntable was ready for use by April 1940 and the FR shed had been demolished by the following year. The outbreak of hostilities caused a postponement in further work, however, and the other sheds (LNWR and MR) remained in use with locomotives being repaired out in the open which was clearly far from satisfactory. The delay lasted for two years or so and the new depot was eventually opened on 18th December 1944. The shed was brick-built with a louvre pattern roof and much of the construction work was undertaken by Italian prisoners of war. In the mid-1950s about half of the allocation comprised Stanier Class 5MT 4-6-0s while Fowler Class 4Fs were also well represented. Towards the end of the steam era Carnforth depot became famous as one of the very last BR sheds to service steam traction and became a place of pilgrimage for many enthusiasts. The shed closed from 5th August 1968 and later became a preservation centre; at the time of writing it is the repair and maintenance headquarters of West Coast Railways Limited. In this picture taken at Carnforth shed on 1st August 1968 the line-up of Stanier 'Black Fives' comprises (from l. to r.) Nos.45055, 45212 and 45318. Two days later No.45212 worked the 8.50pm Preston to Blackpool South (5.05pm *ex*-London Euston) while No.45318 hauled the 9.25pm Preston to Liverpool Exchange (5.25pm *ex*-Glasgow Central), these being the last timetabled BR steam passenger trains in normal service. No.45212 survived into preservation on the Keighley and Worth Valley Railway in West Yorkshire. *David Clark*

The foothills of the Cumbrian mountains. A goods working from Crewe to Carlisle is seen near the site of Burton & Holme station in June 1967; motive power is provided by Stanier Class 5MT No.45252. For the first few miles beyond Carnforth the WCML has a short level section and even a brief downhill stretch which provide no hint for enginemen of the demanding work needed to surmount the banks of Grayrigg and Shap that lie ahead. The former station served two small villages but local residents no doubt found the local buses to be more convenient and the station was closed from 27th March 1950. *Noel Machell*

A portrait of Oxenholme station taken on 10th June 1968, looking northwards. Clearly, judging by the brand new rails and new ballast, the main line tracks had just been relayed at this time, no doubt with the intended speed-up of WCML services in view. The principal station buildings are on the southbound platform while the outer face of the island platform, on the left, was mainly used by Windermere branch trains. The signal box was still in use at this date despite its rather dilapidated condition. Steam traction was still employed northwards on goods workings to Windermere but regular steam workings towards Carlisle had ceased at the end of 1967, apart from the occasional isolated working as far as Shap quarry. The logical route for the WCML northwards from Lancaster would have been up the Lune valley via Kirkby Lonsdale but the citizens of Kendal were vociferous in their demands to have the line routed through their town, apparently regardless of the local topography. In the event the route chosen passed within two miles of Kendal so must be regarded as a compromise, but one achieved at the vast expense of providing banking engines from Oxenholme to Grayrigg. *Tommy Tomalin*

The grind up to Grayrigg summit. A northbound goods train, headed by Stanier 'Royal Scot' Class 7P 4-6-0 No.46141 *The North Staffordshire Regiment,* commences the gruelling climb from Oxenholme up Grayrigg bank, some time in the early 1960s. The pall of smoke at the rear of the train indicates that an assisting locomotive had been provided up the seven miles-long gradient which varied in severity between 1 in 131 and 1 in 106, with the most demanding stretch being the final two miles to the summit. The widespread introduction of English Electric Type 4 diesel locomotives on the WCML rendered many 'Royal Scot' class locomotives redundant and no fewer than 30 examples, almost half of the entire class, were taken out of service in 1962. Those that remained were frequently relegated to menial goods work and were often in disgraceful external condition, as seen here. During its career, No.46141 was allocated to Camden, Bushbury (Wolverhampton) and Carlisle Upperby sheds and was taken out of traffic in April 1964. *RCTS Photo Archive*

A southbound goods working, headed by BR Standard 'Britannia' Pacific No.70014 *Iron Duke*, passes Low Gill on a hazy 30th April 1966. The tracks on the right of the photograph are those of the line to Ingleton which connected with the Carnforth to Skipton line at Clapham. This route lost its regular passenger trains from 1st February 1954 but remained open for diversionary purposes and goods traffic for some years afterwards. There was a station at Low Gill but this was closed from 7th March 1960. In years gone by *Iron Duke* was one of two 'Britannia' Pacifics allocated to Stewarts Lane shed in London for use on the 'Golden Arrow', a prestigious international Pullman car train that connected London and Paris. No.70014 would have been kept in pristine condition for working this train in sad contrast to its deplorable state in this picture. *Tommy Tomalin*

Prior to the construction of the M6 motorway the passage of the Lune gorge was one of the highlights of a journey from London to Scotland and, of course, it offered wonderful opportunities for railway photographers. Here, the photographer has taken full advantage to produce a memorable picture of Stanier 'Princess Coronation' Pacific No.46257 *City of Salford* replenishing its water supply as it passes over Dillicar troughs while hauling an Anglo-Scottish express some time in 1961. Amazingly, the weather conditions were favourable and the valley is bathed in glorious sunshine. The telegraph poles on the extreme right of the picture mark the course of the A685 mountain road that served Tebay while the river Lune is out of sight on the left of the shot. *The late Derek Cross*

The Lake District is famous for its totally unpredictable weather conditions and in this picture menacing, dark clouds hover above the Lune gorge indicating, no doubt, that rain was on its way. The photographer appears to have been extremely fortunate, however, to have captured this northbound goods train in a welcome patch of sunshine as it approached Tebay on an August day in 1966. The locomotive in charge is an unidentified BR Standard 'Britannia' Pacific and, in view of its very heavy train, it would have required the assistance of a banking engine for the ascent of Shap. Unfortunately, the majestic landscape in this area was ruined by the building of the M6 motorway in the late 1960s; the Lancaster to Carlisle section was opened in 1970. *Alan Reeve*

Whilst Tebay was famous among the railway enthusiast community as the location where northbound trains often halted for assistance, the station served only a small village and very few trains stopped for passengers. This picture depicts the 6.00am Warrington (Bank Quay) to Carlisle stopping train arriving behind Stanier 'Black Five' No.45425 on a sunny morning in the summer of 1963. This was one of only three northbound trains that served the station at that time, the others being the 9.25am Crewe to Aberdeen and the Carlisle portion of the 10.40am from Euston which called at Tebay at 5.02pm. The last-mentioned was a multi-portioned service that also conveyed through coaches to Barrow-in-Furness, and Windermere.
*The late Derek Cross*

2nd-SINGLE   SINGLE-2nd

Tebay to

**SHAP**

6512    (M)   1/8   Fare   1/8  (M)    6512

For conditions see over   For conditions see over

The Lancaster and Carlisle Railway built a small engine shed at Loups Fell, about half a mile north of Tebay station, but when the Stainmore line opened in 1861 the LNWR decided that more spacious premises were needed. It built a new depot west of the station which opened during that year; the shed was constructed of stone with a hipped timber-frame roof. During its heyday it boasted an allocation of 28 engines but by the time of the grouping the number of locomotives being maintained there had been reduced to 20. By the mid-1930s the shed was in a woeful condition and virtually roofless, so working at the depot during freezing winter nights must have been extremely unpleasant. The LMSR provided a new water tank in 1943 and, at long last, the shed was rebuilt in 1947/48 including a much-needed new roof. The depot's modernisation was completed by BR in the mid-1950s when a new coal and ash plant were installed plus a 60ft diameter turntable. By this time, however, the shed's duties were mainly banking turns for Fowler 2-6-4Ts, for which it was so well known, and one or two other menial goods workings for 4F Class 0-6-0s. The closure of the line to Barnard Castle in early 1962 further reduced the shed's importance and by the end of 1967, when banking up to Shap summit ceased, only a paltry five BR Standard Class 4MT 4-6-0s remained. The shed is depicted in this picture which was taken on 25th July 1963 with the station platforms in the foreground. *Rodney Lissenden*

In this scene, recorded at Tebay on 8th July 1960, Fairburn Class 4MT 2-6-4T No.42673 'blows off' in the station before departing with the 2.45pm Durham to Ulverston train; the 2-6-4T had just replaced Ivatt Class 2MT 2-6-0 No.46458 that had brought the train across the Pennines from Durham via Barnard Castle. This train, which was not advertised to the general public, ran on alternate Fridays solely for the benefit of miners going to convalesce at either Grange-over-Sands or Ulverston. After traversing the spectacular line over Stainmore summit the train was routed along the Kirkby Stephen to Tebay branch which was used by passenger trains during only the summer period by this date. The train also ran along the obscure Hincaster Junction to Arnside line that lost its regular passenger workings from 1st March 1953, so it was a really fascinating journey. Note the distinctive rows of terraced cottages that were originally constructed for railway workers; the village of Tebay is around half a mile northwards. *John Langford*

In steam days the section of line between Tebay and Shap summit acted like a magnet for lineside photographers and it must be one of the most photographed, perhaps *the* most photographed, stretches of line in Great Britain. But this is another picture taken from an unconventional angle, this time looking towards the WCML from above the tracks of the former line to Kirkby Stephen and Barnard Castle, and is the first shot the author has ever seen taken from that position. An unidentified 2-6-4T locomotive can be seen at the rear of a goods train as it gets to grips with the climb to the summit. Interestingly, the sidings in the foreground appear to have been commandeered as a storage point for redundant rolling stock and the 'hot cross bun' branding indicates that in all likelihood their next stop will be the scrap yard. Perhaps Tebay was chosen because of its remote and relatively isolated position which made it more secure than alternative locations. *The late Derek Cross*

The absorbing ritual of banking up to Shap summit. In this picture an unidentified Hughes/Fowler 6P5F 2-6-0 waits for a banker to buffer-up at the rear of the train before assaulting the climb to Shap summit. The column of smoke being emitted by a 2-6-4T on the right of the photograph indicates that the train will soon be on its way. The bridge just visible towards the rear of the train indicates the course of the river Lune which, for a short distance, has been on the west side of the railway. The line of wagons marks the position of the line to Kirkby Stephen from which regular passenger services were withdrawn in December 1952, although seasonal trains continued until September 1961. *Rodney Lissenden*

A further view of the line in the Tebay area that is refreshingly different to those normally seen. Here, a clean Stanier Class 8F 2-8-0, hauling a long train of vanfits, comes down the bank towards Tebay on 30th June 1964. Luckily, the fireman had just placed a shovelful of coal onto the fire or, perhaps, the driver had just put the blower on, thus giving a bit of life to the picture. Note the meandering river Lune on the right. The M6 motorway now crosses the line in this vicinity and has completely devastated this once relatively peaceful location. *Rodney Lissenden*

Summer at Greenholme. An unknown BR Standard 'Britannia' Pacific climbs past Greenholme with a goods working some time during the summer of 1964. This was an easily accessible spot for lineside photographers and, of course, the backdrop was breathtaking. The locomotive is 'blowing off' so clearly had plenty of steam available for the rest of the ascent to Shap summit and, judging by the lack of smoke at the rear of the train, it seems to be tackling the climb single-handed. *Alan Reeve*

Winter at Greenholme. You can almost feel the penetrating cold in this portrait of Stanier Class 5MT No.44753 powering up to Shap summit with a goods train during the winter of 1963. Full marks to the intrepid photographer for venturing out in such snowy and inhospitable conditions! The locomotive seen here is of particular interest, being one of only 20 members of its class fitted with Caprotti valve gear, a high pitched boiler and low running plates which gave them a very distinctive appearance. Even their best friends would not have called these locomotives handsome! No.44753 was built at Crewe in March 1948 but had a relatively short working life compared to other members of the class, being withdrawn in July 1965. No.44753 was actually one of the last survivors of this variant, most being taken out of service in 1963/64; perhaps they had been deemed to be non-standard and therefore slated for early withdrawal. *RCTS Photo Archive*

A stirring and evocative shot of 'Princess Coronation' Pacific No.46229 *Duchess of Hamilton* apparently making good progress on the climb to Shap summit with the northbound 'Royal Scot' which was the crack daytime train on this route at the time; this picture was taken near Scout Green on 8th September 1956. The 'Royal Scot' was introduced in 1927 and by the summer of 1939 the down train offered a journey time of seven hours from London to Glasgow. Then came the interruption for the Second World War but afterwards a slow improvement in journey times followed, although never quite attaining the pre-war standard. In 1958 schedules started to be affected by engineering works for electrification and were artificially inflated to allow for this work. *Bob Leslie/Peter Robinson collection*

Generations of railway photographers have complained about the fickle and totally unpredictable weather conditions in the area of Shap summit where weather forecasts always seemed to be wholly inaccurate. But here the fells are bathed in glorious sunshine offering incontrovertible evidence that it did not always rain on Shap! Despite its grimy external condition Stanier Class 5MT 4-6-0 No.45072 appears to be making a confident climb to the summit without a trace of leaking steam at the front end; a 2-6-4T locomotive is providing a welcome 'push' at the rear of the train. Note the assortment of rolling stock forming the train which consists of two Gresley-designed coaches immediately behind the engine while the rest comprises a mixture of BR Standard and LMSR-designed vehicles. This picture was taken near Scout Green on 26th July 1963. *Martin Smith*

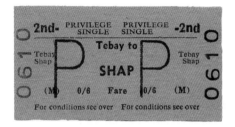

Shap Wells was a favourite photographic spot where there was a field that provided an ideal grandstand from where to observe and photograph trains battling up the bank from Tebay. Sometimes, if a locomotive was in poor condition, a train could take as much as 20 minutes to complete the climb but, while this may have been an ordeal for the locomotive's crew, it simply added to the enjoyment of lineside spectators. Here, an unidentified Stanier Class 8F 2-8-0, assisted at the rear by a 2-6-4T, plods up the incline towards Shap summit on a hazy April day in 1967. *Alan Reeve*

The run-down of BR steam traction was marked by many particularly sad events but, perhaps, one of the saddest of all was when, in September 1964, the LMR headquarters decreed that all remaining 'Princess Coronation' Pacifics were to be withdrawn from service. Nineteen members of the class were left in running stock at the end of March 1964, all of which were in traffic except for No.46226 *Duchess of Norfolk* which was stored unserviceable at Carlisle Kingmoor shed with a cracked frame. During the summer their duties tended to be irregular and consisted to a large degree of deputising for diesels and working goods and parcels trains. During their last few weeks of activity the 11.30am Birmingham to Edinburgh was noted on 1st September with No.46243 *City of Lancaster* in charge while No.46239 *City of Chester* powered the 10.30am Euston to Carlisle on 7th September. The 4th of September saw the final workings of the 'Caledonian' and the down train produced No.46238 *City of Carlisle* – a veritable swan song if ever there was one! All survivors were due to be taken out of service on 12th September, with the exception of No.46256 *Sir William A. Stanier F.R.S.* which was required for a Railway Correspondence and Travel Society special train at the end of the month. Here, No.46254 *City of Stoke-on-Trent* is seen at Shap Wells in August 1964 in charge of the 12.50pm Euston to Glasgow train during its final few days in service. The locomotive was hauling eleven coaches up the bank unassisted and is 'blowing off' furiously – what a way to go! The diagonal yellow stripe on the cab side indicates that the locomotive was not permitted to work south of Crewe due to restricted overhead live wire clearances. *Martin Smith*

Even during the closing years of steam traction on the West Coast Main Line there was no shortage of variety of motive power and in this portrait 'Patriot' Class 7P 4-6-0 No.45545 *Planet* appears to be making an effortless climb up the 1 in 75 gradient hauling a substantial ten-coach train; this shot was taken in August 1963. No.45545 was originally built at Crewe in March 1934 but was one of 18 engines of this class extensively rebuilt during the Ivatt regime. The rebuilds were based on the successful modification of two 'Jubilee' class engines in 1942 and were fitted with larger tapered boilers, double chimneys and new cylinders; this work was carried out between 1946 and 1949. *Planet* was taken out of traffic in June 1964 and by the end of that year only three of these rebuilt 'Patriot' locomotives survived in service. One can only imagine the deafening blast from the chimney of No.45545 as it made its way steadily to the summit. *Martin Smith*

Some trains took on a pilot engine at Oxenholme, but these seemed to be the exception rather than the rule; presumably footplate crews on an ailing locomotive sometimes thought it a better option for a pilot to assist them over both the Grayrigg and Shap inclines. In this picture Fairburn Class 4MT 2-6-4T No.42198 gives a Stanier 'Black Five' a helping hand up the bank with a heavy 12-coach formation on 28th June 1964; certainly the pilot engine does not seem to be short of steam. *Rodney Lissenden*

The long, uphill slog from Carlisle is over for the crew of Stanier 'Jubilee' Class 6P5F 4-6-0 No.45593 *Kolhapur* and they can now take it relatively easy as their train gathers momentum downhill towards Tebay on 20th July 1963. No.45593 was allocated to Aston (Birmingham) shed at this time and was subsequently transferred to Patricroft depot, near Manchester. Later in its career *Kolhapur* gained celebrity status when it became one of the last surviving members of its class based at Holbeck shed in Leeds, and some of its final duties included working summer Saturday trains over the Settle and Carlisle line with which the class was so closely identified. When No.45593 was withdrawn from traffic in October 1967 it was sold for preservation at the Birmingham Railway Museum, Tyseley. This is one of the few pictures submitted for publication in this book that included Shap Summit signal box, which seems to have eluded most photographers. This must have been a very busy box, particularly on summer Saturdays when extra trains ran, and finding pathways for banking engines returning to Tebay must have placed considerable strain on the signalman in addition to dealing with the ordinary traffic. *Rodney Lissenden*

Naturally, northbound trains were the principal focus of attention at Shap but here is another photograph of a southbound train. Stanier 'Jubilee' 4-6-0 No.45655 *Keith* eases into the loop line just before Shap summit signal box with a goods train on sunny 25th July 1963. Presumably an express was following close behind and *Keith* was 'looped' to enable it to overtake. The majority of these locomotives were built at Crewe but No.45655 was an exception, being one of a small batch constructed at Derby. This particular machine was out-shopped in December 1934 and lasted in service until April 1965. *Martin Smith*

The 32 miles-long section of the WCML between Carnforth and Shap summit was unquestionably one of toughest stretches on any main line in England, culminating in the gruelling 1 in 75 climb from Greenholme to the summit. The maroon Shap summit sign, which indicated the height above sea level, was always a most welcome sight for enginemen. The sign is seen here in this photograph which was taken on 22nd April 1962. *Martin Smith*

The 30 miles-long southbound climb from Carlisle up to Shap summit is not as steep as the northbound ascent but, even so, involves sections graded at 1 in 125/131 without a respite apart from a few relatively level miles around Penrith where there are even two very brief downhill stretches. Here, the crew of Fowler Class 4F 0-6-0 No.44061 seem to be having a real struggle on their hands with quite a heavy train and the locomotive, emitting a huge pall of smoke across the fells, was apparently making heavy weather of the climb past Hardendale quarry. One wonders whether the crew sought refuge in the loop at the summit. *Martin Smith*

This picture was taken at Shap station on 22nd July 1963. Note that the station platforms appear to have been lit solely by oil lamps so it must have been quite an experience for passengers alighting here on a wet and windy night. At least there was a footbridge so they did not have to cross the main line tracks in the dark! Shap probably had the poorest service of any station on the WCML and the winter 1964/65 timetable listed only two northbound weekday trains, one in the morning and one in the evening, the latter being a very slow through working from London. In the reverse direction there were trains at 7.17am to Crewe and 8.03pm to Warrington and these were supplemented by a through train to London at the more convenient time of 9.31am; the last mentioned was booked to arrive at Euston at 4.20pm so was hardly designed to cater for passengers wanting a day out in the capital! *Rodney Lissenden*

A view of Shap station, showing Stanier Class 5MT 4-6-0 No.44677 passing through with (what appears to be) a southbound civil engineer's train on 8th August 1967. Situated in a wild and windswept location at 850 feet above sea level the station was the highest between Carnforth and Carlisle; it was solidly built and possessed a modest platform canopy on the northbound side while a waiting shelter sufficed on the southbound platform. The station was closed, together with Milnthorpe and Tebay, from 1st July 1968 when the stopping trains between Carnforth and Carlisle were withdrawn. Penrith and Oxenholme, of course, continued to be served by main line express services. *Tommy Tomalin*

Photographed against the backdrop of the wooded slopes of Beaconhill, Stanier Class 5MT 4-6-0 No.45148 pulls away from Penrith with a southbound goods train on 29th June 1965; the locomotive's crew have ensured that their engine will not run out of coal during the journey! Judging by the number of wagons present the goods yard seems to have been busy at this time. Note the position of the locomotive's top headcode lamp; the top lamp bracket used to be above the smokebox door but the installation of overhead live wires, in connection with the electrification of the WCML, created a serious hazard for locomotive crews and it was re-positioned as depicted here to avoid accidents. *Bob Leslie/Peter Robinson collection*

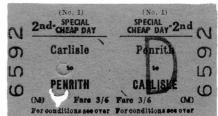

George Hughes was the Chief Mechanical Engineer (CME) of the Lancashire and Yorkshire Railway from 1904 to 1921 and became CME of the LMSR in 1923. He is probably best remembered for his class of 6P5F 2-6-0s, the first of which appeared from Horwich works in May 1926 after he had left office and been replaced by Sir Henry Fowler, so the entire class of 245 locomotives was built under Fowler's jurisdiction, the final example appearing in December 1932. The 2-6-0s were commonly referred to as 'Crabs' due to their distinctive high running plates and angle of the cylinders. They may have looked rather awkward but this was not reflected in their performance and these engines had an excellent reputation due to their sure-footed characteristics which made life much easier for enginemen, particularly in wet conditions. Here, a group of train spotters appears to be transfixed as No.42788 makes steady progress through Penrith station with a southbound goods train on 26th July 1963. This engine was allocated to Gorton shed at the time of the photograph, so perhaps it was bound for the Manchester area. *Martin Smith*

Every railway photographer dreams of the classic combination of sunshine and snow and here the elements combine perfectly to produce a dazzling picture of Stanier Class 5MT No.45376 heading southwards at Kitchenhill, just a few miles north of Penrith. No.45376 appears to have steam to spare at this point where the gradients are moderate, but sterner work lies ahead once Penrith has been passed. This picture was taken in 1966. *Bob Leslie/Peter Robinson collection*

Apart from a handful of main line diesel locomotives, steam reigned supreme on the WCML in the 1950s and here is a classic view of the 13-coach London-bound 'Mid-Day Scot' near Plumpton on 9th July 1955; motive power is provided by Stanier Class 8P 'Princess Royal' Pacific No.46210 *Lady Patricia*. Unfortunately, No.46210 later became one of the first Stanier Pacifics to be taken out of service. All of the class were put into store as 'surplus to requirements' in early 1961 and No.46210 was stored unserviceable at Carlisle Kingmoor shed from about March. About half of the class, however, re-emerged at the start of the summer timetable but *Lady Patricia* was not among them and remained on the stored line at the depot. It was among six members of the class withdrawn in October 1961, one of the first victims of the widespread introduction of main line diesels on the WCML. *Bob Leslie/Peter Robinson collection*

Trains heading southwards from Carlisle immediately faced a gradient of almost four miles at 1 in 131 and enginemen are hardly likely to have relished the prospect of tackling this incline with a 'cold' engine. In this illustration, 'Royal Scot' Class 7P 4-6-0 No.46132 *The King's Regiment Liverpool* seems to be making good headway with a van train on 11th May 1963. The building on the right of the shot is the former Brisco station, located about five miles south of Carlisle, which was closed only six years after the line opened, being replaced by nearby Wreay station. The latter, which served only a small hamlet, was a wartime casualty, closing from 16th August 1943. *Bob Leslie/Peter Robinson collection*

Super power on the West Coast Main Line. A massive 14-coach Glasgow (Central) to Manchester (Victoria) train approaches the former Brisco station on 4th July 1959; motive power is provided by 'Jubilee' Class 6P5F 4-6-0 No.45668 *Madden* piloting 'Royal Scot' Class 7P 4-6-0 No.46102 *Black Watch*. At that period the journey time from Glasgow to Manchester was around six hours and the 4.05pm from the Scottish city was due to arrive in Manchester at 10.01pm. This train also conveyed through carriages from both Glasgow and Edinburgh to Liverpool (Exchange) but not, apparently, through coaches from Edinburgh to Manchester; the restaurant car went through to Manchester. *Bob Leslie/Peter Robinson collection*

On Whit Monday, 3rd June 1963, BR laid on a special train from Carlisle to Blackpool and, despite the large number of diesels that would presumably have been available on a bank holiday, steam traction in the shape of 'Black Five' No.44937 from Upperby shed was rostered, and it is seen here setting off from the border city in fine style. At the time of this photograph goods traffic normally by-passed the station on the goods lines located on the western side of the city; trains from all directions were able to access these by virtue of improvements completed in 1878. The rear part of the train seen here is passing over the low-level goods tracks which considerably reduced congestion around the station. The tightly curved tracks on the right which descend towards the goods lines are used by services on the Newcastle and Settle routes. On the left the line from Workington, which like the WCML also passes over the goods tracks on a bridge, can just be discerned. Carlisle station can be seen in the background on the right of the photograph with the city's distinctive skyline beyond. Let us hope that the passengers had a really enjoyable day out at Blackpool. *Bob Leslie/Peter Robinson collection*

Portrait of a fading star. The mass invasion of the WCML by English Electric Type 4 diesels in the early 1960s naturally reduced the work of the steam fleet and the first victims among the elite express passenger locomotives were six Stanier 'Princess Royal' Class 8P Pacifics which (as previously mentioned) were taken out of service at the end of the summer 1961 timetable. No.46200 *The Princess Royal,* like other members of the class, had spent a period in store in early 1961 and was returned to storage at the end of the summer timetable but not withdrawn. Predictably, perhaps, there was a motive power shortage in early 1962 and all six surviving 'Princess Royal' Pacifics re-entered service with No.46200 being allocated to Carlisle Upperby shed in company with sister engines Nos.46201/3, but in April they were moved to nearby Kingmoor shed. *The Princess Royal* was very active and appeared on the 'Aberdeen Flyer' rail tour on 3rd June, the 9.35am Wolverhampton (High Level) to Euston on

the following day and the 9.50am Euston to Perth, presumably from Carlisle, on 8th June. But time was running out for this celebrated class and in October 1962 the withdrawal orders were issued for the remaining six engines, but No.46200 continued at work for a few more weeks becoming the last active survivor in normal traffic. Initially, it was stored at Kingmoor following withdrawal but was moved to Upperby shed at some stage and was photographed there, looking rather forlorn, on 13th June 1964 by which time its paintwork was fading badly after prolonged exposure to the elements. *Rodney Lissenden*

A Glasgow to Manchester (Victoria) train headed by 'Patriot' Class 6P5F 4-6-0 No.45537 *Private E. Sykes V.C.* makes a smoky exit from Carlisle Citadel station on 3rd August 1953. Note the lower quadrant signals and generally dilapidated state of the premises following years of war-time neglect. The first railway to reach the city was the Newcastle and Carlisle Railway which opened a station at London Road in 1836, and in the mid-1840s the Maryport and Carlisle, Lancaster and Carlisle and Caledonian railways successively added lines from other points of the compass. The Glasgow and South Western Railway followed in 1850 and the North British Railway opened its route from Edinburgh in 1862. Traffic grew considerably and the multiplicity of goods yards meant that day-to-day operation was becoming increasingly difficult despite piecemeal improvements, and the inadequate facilities were acutely overloaded. The impending arrival of the Midland Railway (MR) from Leeds prompted a massive investment in new goods avoiding lines around the city and a reorganisation of passenger tracks to reduce congestion and ease the flow. Carlisle Citadel station was greatly enlarged with a new island platform and overall roof covering seven acres. The MR arrived in Carlisle in 1876 when its epic route across the Pennines was finally completed but, despite the improvements, there was still considerable duplication of goods and locomotive facilities which entailed much wasteful trip working between the various yards. The problems can be gauged from the fact that in 1922 there were eleven separate goods yards within the city boundary and it is hardly surprising that a substantial number of local inhabitants were employed on the railway. The much-needed rationalisation of Carlisle's goods yards took place in 1963 when a new marshalling yard opened north of the city, but it can be argued that this installation was already out of date when it was commissioned and contraction started as early as 1972. One of the foremost suppliers of railway equipment, Cowans Sheldon, whose products were despatched across the globe, was based in Carlisle. The end of steam in the city in 1967, and the sad closure of the Waverley route to Edinburgh in January 1969, caused a reduction in the number of goods lines and closure of maintenance depots around the city but, even today, Carlisle remains one of the most absorbing railway centres in Great Britain. *Bob Leslie/Peter Robinson collection*

The great days at Carlisle. Two giants of steam, LMSR 'Princess Coronation' Pacific No.46250 *City of Lichfield* and LNER Class A3 Pacific No.60037 *Hyperion* stand at the south end of the station in the early 1950s. No.60037 was based at Haymarket shed, Edinburgh, during this period and had presumably worked south over the Waverley route, while No.46250 was doubtless waiting to take over a London-bound express. Many trains changed engines at Carlisle, thus making it a very rewarding centre for enthusiasts. Note that the station roof, which dated from 1880, appears to be close to disintegration and it was not before time when it was replaced in the mid-1950s. *RCTS Photo Archive*

Carlisle station was famous for heavy express passenger trains making a noisy and smoky departure but here in total contrast is a really peaceful scene, perhaps taken during a lull in traffic, depicting a pair of LMSR Class 3F 0-6-0Ts engaged on station pilot work at the southern end of the premises. No.47377 stands on one of the middle roads with a string of coaches, the one nearest to the camera being a Royal Mail van in its colourful livery, while sister locomotive No.47347 takes water. These unsung shunting engines were affectionately known as 'Jinties'. *RCTS Photo Archive*

Steam traction in everyday service in the border city came to an end, as previously mentioned, in 1967 and to mark the close of the steam era Kingmoor shed turned out immaculate BR Standard 'Britannia' Pacific No.70013 *Oliver Cromwell* to haul a football special to and from Blackpool – one wonders whether many of the fans appreciated the historical significance of this grand finale. The *very* last steam working from Carlisle was the 1.10pm goods to Skipton on 30th December headed by sister engine No.70045 *Lord Rowallan*. During the late 1960s many people still took their summer break at British resorts – the lure of the Spanish beaches was still relatively unknown – and in 1967 many Saturday holiday trains ran to popular resorts such as Blackpool which was a favourite with many Scots. These additional workings placed considerable strain on motive power resources and, as a result, there was a fair amount of steam working along the WCML north of Preston. In this picture, taken at Carlisle on 5th August 1967, Stanier Class 5MT 4-6-0 No.44911 clearly has plenty of steam in reserve for the demanding work ahead as it departs with the 11.05am SO Glasgow (Central) to Blackpool (North) train. Two young boys look on in awe as the locomotive gets its train on the move. On the left of the picture, standing on one of the middle roads, is No.44802 which is waiting to take over the 9.10am SO Dundee to Blackpool train; this was due to depart from Carlisle at 1.57pm, nine minutes after the working from Glasgow. It may, at first glance, seem strange that the train from Dundee, that departed from there almost two hours before the one from Glasgow, left Carlisle later but this is explained by the fact that the Dundee train travelled over the Waverley route and therefore had a much longer journey. The passengers had plenty of time to think about the prospect of spending a fortnight by the sea, the scheduled arrival time at Blackpool being 4.41pm, just in time for a lavish five-course evening meal at their chosen guest house! *The late Derek Cross*

The attractive frontage of Carlisle station, designed by Sir William Tite in the Tudor style, is depicted in this picture taken in 1964; the building is, of course, listed as a structure of particular architectural interest. Trains from the capital used London Road station until the new premises were opened on 1st September 1847. The station was known as 'Carlisle Citadel' for many years, taking its name from nearby law courts in the form of two large towers based on Henry VIII's citadel; they were completed by Sir Robert Smirke in 1811. Note the Royal arms of the Lancaster & Carlisle Railway above the main entrance and also that of the Caledonian Railway which contributed £100,000 and £64,000 respectively to construction costs of the new station. Two other spaces were provided for the arms of the Newcastle & Carlisle and Maryport & Carlisle companies but they apparently failed to honour an agreement for the joint working of the station and were left blank. Perhaps the most impressive feature of Carlisle station's exterior is the clock tower. In its heyday no fewer than seven companies used the station and the daily procession of trains in almost every livery imaginable must have been dazzling. There is a small square in front of the station with floral displays and, at least at the time of this photograph(!), a magnificent collection of cars and vans that would qualify as valuable collectors' pieces today. *Stuart Ackley collection*

A shot taken at the north end of Carlisle station showing Stanier Class 5MT 4-6-0 No.45279 departing with a relief to the northbound 'Thames-Clyde Express' on 5th August 1967. Note that there are three diesel locomotives just in view beyond the road bridge. During the summer of 1967 steam traction was out in full force on summer Saturday dated trains on both the Shap and Settle & Carlisle lines and yet, a mere five months after this picture was taken, this form of motive power was totally eliminated from the area and diesel traction was in full control. *The late Derek Cross*

The West Coast Main Line crosses the river Eden about two miles north of Carlisle at Etterby and in this illustration Stanier Class 5MT 4-6-0 No.45177 is seen powering a northbound goods train on 11th August 1962. This was always a favourite location for railway photographers and spotters who congregated on the bridge overlooking the tracks after a visit to Kingmoor motive power depot, just a few hundred yards away on the other side of the roadbridge. In addition to a fine gantry signal and distant outline of the city skyline, this spot also provided a good view of the two railway bridges across the river. The structure furthest away from the camera is the original bridge while the nearer one, which carries the goods lines across the river, was constructed during the Second World War, presumably to eliminate a bottleneck and speed-up the movement of equipment needed for the war effort. *Bob Leslie/Peter Robinson collection*

A scene photographed at the northern end of Hellifield station showing BR Standard Class 9F No.92233 approaching with a heavy Long Meg to Widnes train of anhydrite in June 1965. Despite its relatively isolated and rather bleak location, Hellifield's junction status ensured it was always reasonably busy and, in addition, it was the starting/terminating point for one or two local trains to and from Carlisle. The engine shed at Hellifield was some distance from the village and, following closure as an operational depot, was used by the Curator of Historical Relics as a store for locomotives scheduled for preservation as part of the National Collection.
*RCTS Photo Archive*

The down 'Waverley', with Gresley Class A3 Pacific No.60072 *Sunstar* in charge, accelerates away from its Hellifield station stop on 27th June 1961. In the summer 1959 timetable 'The Waverley' left St Pancras at 9.10am and ran non-stop to Nottingham before reaching Leeds (City) at 1.48pm. The train then continued to Carlisle, calling at Skipton, Hellifield, and Appleby, its arrival time in the border city being 4.14pm. Passengers travelling from, say, Nottingham to Galashiels would have been faced with an almost seven hour, marathon journey but at least the train's formation included a restaurant car so they would have been able to enjoy a meal on board and, of course, after Skipton the scenery was breathtaking. 'The Waverley' eventually arrived in Edinburgh at 6.55pm on Mondays to Fridays (7.17pm on Saturdays). *Gavin Morrison*

The Settle and Carlisle (S&C) line starts at Settle Junction, where the line to Carnforth diverges, and in this portrait immaculate Stanier Class 5MT 4-6-0 No.45390 is seen posing at Settle Junction whilst in the course of working the 1.05pm Carnforth to Skipton goods on 2nd August 1968. The locomotive's superb external condition was probably the result of cleaning by enthusiasts at Carnforth shed during the last few days of regular BR steam workings and, indeed, it is likely that this train was the *very* last ordinary BR steam working past Settle Junction. The history of the famous S&C line has been very well documented over the years and it is probably true to say that few lines have captured the imagination of railway enthusiasts as much as this epic route, so perhaps only a brief outline of its history is appropriate here. The Midland Railway (MR) had ambitious plans to carry traffic from the Midlands to Scotland and acquired various small, independent companies operating north of Leeds, and it hoped to send its Scottish traffic via Ingleton from where a connection to the Lancaster and Carlisle Railway's (L&CR) route was available. When the MR tried to negotiate with the rival London & North Western Railway (LNWR), successor to the L&CR, it proved to be very obstructive and ruled out any possibility of through running to Carlisle. The MR was forced to think again and in the 1866 parliamentary session proposed a line from Settle to Carlisle with a branch to Hawes and, despite vehement opposition from the LNWR, this was approved and received the Royal assent on 16th July 1866. The LNWR, having failed to keep the MR out of Carlisle, then moderated its opposition and offered easier access to the Border city so the MR considered abandoning the S&C project, but this angered other railway companies who hoped to benefit from the MR's expansion and its proposal to abandon the line was rejected by Parliament. Some people may argue that was one of the most enlightened decisions ever taken by Parliament! The MR was left with no option but to proceed and four contracts were let for the construction of the main route with a fifth for the Hawes branch; the first sod was cut at Anley, near Settle, in November 1869. The contractors, however, had not appreciated the wild and inhospitable terrain through which they had to drive the line, nor had they realised quite how ferocious the weather could be high up on the northern fells. During the period of construction up to 7,000 men were employed at any one time and it was a continually changing labour force because some navvies left due to the dreadful winter weather conditions while in the summer others were attracted to less arduous work in the fields gathering the harvest. The men were housed in basic hutted encampments on the high fells and tales abounded of disease and drunken brawls; not all survived the harsh conditions and were laid to rest in the churchyard at Chapel-le-Dale, between Ribblehead and Ingleton. The legendary S&C route was opened to goods traffic in August 1875 but, surprisingly, when the first through MR train to Scotland left St Pancras on 1st May 1876 there was no ceremony at all. BR's attempt to shut the line in the 1980s provoked widespread protests and today the line is a cherished national asset, offering unbeatable vistas of the breathtaking Pennine landscape. *David Clark*

An engineman's view of the 'Long Drag'. The arduous 15 miles-long climb from Settle Junction to Blea Moor was known to railwaymen as the 'Long Drag' and this picture provides a fascinating insight into how it looked from the footplate. This shot was taken from the cab of Gresley Class A3 Pacific No.60082 *Neil Gow* as it approached Settle station hauling 'The Thames-Clyde Express' on 30th April 1961. What a memorable experience this journey must have been for the photographer but for the engine's crew it was just a routine, day-in, day-out job along a line they had travelled many times. In the summer 1959 timetable this train was booked non-stop from Leeds (City) to Carlisle, the departure time from Leeds being 2.46pm while the train's scheduled arrival time at the border city was 5.04pm. *Gavin Morrison*

Between Settle and Stainforth the S&C line threads a deep gorge running side-by-side with the foaming and tumbling waters of the river Ribble but after Stainforth the landscape opens out, the first point of interest being Helwith Bridge. Here, there was a signal box, dating from August 1896, that controlled the entrance to the Ribblesdale Lime Company's sidings. There was also a ground frame for the Helwith Bridge Granite Company siding which was released by a lever in the signal box. The siding was taken out of use on 7th September 1969, from which date the ground frame and signal box were also closed. The latter company's conveyor, which crossed the river, can be discerned in the background of this shot of the lengthy 1.27pm Wigan (North Western) to Carlisle van train heading north on a miserable 29th April 1967; the train had been diverted via the S&C line due to bridge works in the Penrith area in connection with the construction of the M6 motorway. Motive power is provided by BR Standard 'Britannia' Pacific No.70032 *Tennyson* piloting train engine, 'Black Five' No.44674. *Ron Herbert*

The fells in the background appear to be shrouded in mist when this picture of the colourful signs at Horton-in-Ribblesdale station was taken in July 1965, leaving alighting passengers in no doubt regarding the station's location. Passengers on northbound trains had another 65 miles of glorious Pennine scenery to look forward to – provided the mist cleared, of course. *Alan Reeve*

Low cloud hides the top of Whernside (2,419 feet above sea level) as Stanier 'Black Five' No.44684 passes Ribblehead station on a gloomy 26th July 1966. The station building is particularly interesting because the end walls and projecting gables have been tiled to keep out the worst of the weather conditions. Various names were originally suggested for the station, including Ingleton Road and Batty Green, but Ribblehead was eventually selected apparently after the intervention of a local clergyman. A set of points south of the down platform gave access to a private siding which was laid in 1945, entry being controlled from the adjacent signal box; the box was closed from 17th August 1969. Whilst the station may have been used only by the most hardy and determined traveller, it doubled as a meteorological station (note the anemometer on the pole) and the stationmaster and his staff were trained to compile and despatch weather reports to the Meteorological Office on an hourly basis, so they were kept busy. The frequency of the reports may seem unjustifiable to the casual observer but in the author's opinion this was quite sensible, bearing in mind the rapid and unpredictable variations in weather conditions at Ribblehead. In times gone by strong winds have ripped tarpaulins off wagons formed in trains crossing Batty Moss viaduct. *Tommy Tomalin*

On 11th August 1968 the curtain came down on BR steam traction, the end being commemorated by a rail tour from Liverpool to Carlisle and back, routed via the Settle and Carlisle line. Here, 'Black Five' Nos. 44781 and 44871 are pictured coming off Ribblehead viaduct and starting the long descent to Settle Junction. The train's appearance fortunately coincided with a patch of sunlight as it passed the photographer's viewpoint, the background being in shadow. *RCTS Photo Archive*

The perfect morning at Ribblehead. Notorious for its hostile climate, the weather conditions at Ribblehead are not always bad and the morning of 26th August 1966 was bright and calm. Imagine the photographer's huge joy, therefore, when this northbound goods train was signalled and, no doubt after a long wait, Stanier 'Jubilee' Class 6P5F 4-6-0 No.45697 *Achilles* hove into view making slow but steady progress across Batty Moss viaduct with a heavy goods train. Note the top of Ingleborough is partially obscured by cloud. Usually in these ideal conditions a tiny cloud appears, hiding the sun at just the wrong moment, but on this occasion luck was on the photographer's side and this masterpiece resulted. Wonderful!
*Roy Hobbs*

The swan song of the 'Jubilees'. Following the end of steam on the Southern Region on 9th July 1967, the only remaining express passenger locomotives in BR service were a stud of BR Standard 'Britannia' Pacifics and a small number of Stanier 'Jubilee' Class 6P5F 4-6-0s allocated to Holbeck shed, Leeds. During the summer the 6.40am SO Birmingham (New Street) to Glasgow and 9.20am SO St Pancras to Glasgow were rostered for 'Jubilee' haulage and naturally attracted many enthusiasts who travelled on the trains or photographed them from the lineside. Some photographers made the long trek from the south of England or Midlands only to be greeted by the grim conditions seen in this picture of No.45593 *Kolhapur* approaching Blea Moor in August 1967. Other people were more fortunate, however, and experienced better conditions more conducive to photography – it was all a question of luck. *Alan Reeve*

Almost there! After almost 14 miles of tough climbing up the 'Long Drag' from Settle the crew of BR Standard Class 9F 2-10-0 No. 92223, hauling a train of empty anhydrite wagons returning to Long Meg, have only a mile to go to the summit, which is located just inside Blea Moor tunnel (2,629 yards long). Another, unidentified, member of the same class, in charge of a loaded Long Meg to Widnes train, sits in the up loop taking water; this picture was taken during the summer of 1967. Originally, Blea Moor signal box was on the down side but was replaced in 1941 when the old lie-by sidings were superseded by passing loops; the new box, which was brought into use on 20th September 1941, is visible above the rear of the southbound goods train. The signal box at Blea Moor was a particularly isolated and lonely outpost, so if a goods train stopped for water, or was held in a loop to allow a passenger train to pass, this became something of a social occasion for the signalman who was able to chat with the train crew and, perhaps, if time permitted, brew them a fresh cup of tea. In stark contrast when the line was being constructed the area around Blea Moor was home to hundreds of navvies who lived in a large shanty town constructed on bare moorland at Batty Green, at the point where Ribblehead viaduct was to be built. There were workshops and wooden huts for the men who, at the peak of the construction work, numbered 2,000. They laid over two miles of tramway from the turnpike road at Ribblehead to what was to be the southern entrance to Blea Moor tunnel. The characteristics of America's wild west seem to have taken hold in the dales and bare fist fights, fuelled by excessive drinking, resulted in the MR recruiting a local scripture reader, James Tiplady, who preached in the open and his 'parish' extended along 17 miles of railway. This gentleman apparently had the benefit of a free pass which entitled him to travel from Settle to Bradford once a month but history has not recorded whether his teachings moderated the behaviour of the more aggressive navvies. *Alan Reeve*

Lovely puffy clouds scud across the sky as an unidentified BR Standard Class 9F 2-10-0 sets off from Blea Moor's down loop with a northbound train of hopper wagons, presumably 'empties' returning to Long Meg sidings, near Lazonby; this shot dates from about July 1965. The water tank on the right is understood to date from 1941 when loops were installed. Blea Moor signal box is obscured by the tank and the only other buildings visible are adjacent to the box, these being a pair of MR cottages and a more modern house. The atrocious weather in this area can be gauged by the fact that the highest ground can have 70 inches of rain a year while a record annual fall at Ribblehead occurred in 1954 when no less than 109½ inches were recorded. It is not unheard of for snow to be found in shady pockets as late as June. Unsurprisingly, the weather, arduous work and disease took its toll of the navvies, many of whom, as previously mentioned, were laid to rest in the churchyard at Chapel-le-Dale between Ribblehead and Ingleton; sadly the churchyard had to be enlarged to accommodate the many victims. *Alan Reeve*

Located in the beautiful surroundings of Dentdale, Arten Gill viaduct is widely considered to be the most graceful on the S&C line and in this portrait taken in August 1967 BR Standard 'Britannia' Pacific No.70024 *Vulcan* is depicted crossing this impressive structure with a northbound goods train. The viaduct was constructed of Dent marble, a limestone with white fossils, which was quarried locally as its name suggests; work commenced on 3rd May 1871 and the 220 yards-long structure was built over a period of four years. The viaduct is 117ft above the valley floor at its highest point. *Author*

Understandably perhaps, BR's expectations of the traffic potential of the wayside stations on the S&C line were low and the basic service was not generous, consisting of two return trains a day supplemented by short workings between Carlisle and Appleby. The morning trains started/terminated at Hellifield of all places but the afternoon workings were more useful and ran to and from Bradford (Forster Square). In 1965 these trains were still steam worked, usual motive power being a 'Black Five' or, occasionally, a BR Standard 'Clan' Pacific; four of the latter were still allocated to Carlisle (Kingmoor) shed in mid-1965 though their ranks were reduced to just two survivors by the end of the year. In this photograph, taken on a gloriously sunny evening in July 1965, No.72008 *Clan Macleod* pulls away from Dent station with the 4.37pm Carlisle to Bradford (Forster Square) train. Note the snow fences on the fell-side, these being built in an attempt to stop the worst of the winter snow from drifting on to the track; also the waiting shelter on the up platform was recessed into the hillside. Dent was roughly the halfway point on the marathon, almost four hours-long journey between the two cities but on a clear evening the scenery was absolutely breathtaking and more than adequate compensation for the time spent travelling. *Alan Reeve*

*Clan Macleod* sets off from Dent station with the train seen in the previous picture; it is the highest main line station in England at 1,145 feet above sea level. Dent signal box dated from 9th August 1891 and had a 20 lever frame; it was taken out of commission on 28th January 1981. Situated on a ledge above Dentdale, the station is approached from the valley by a crazy corkscrew road, known locally as the 'coal road', which continues over the fells and eventually descends to Garsdale station; it climbs over 450 feet in half a mile to reach Dent station. The 'coal road' was originally

built to serve coal pits, long since defunct, on Widdale fell. The station is about four miles from the village and travellers arriving there without transport are faced with a long trek, not an inviting prospect on a wild, Pennine night. Dent station was not opened until 1877, the delay being caused because the MR could not decide on a location that had the support of the local people. Various sites were suggested including, bizarrely, sites adjacent to Dent Head and Arten Gill viaducts. The former would have been seven miles from the village while the latter would have required such a steep approach that only the fittest of dales folk would have been able to reach it without assistance! *Alan Reeve*

A winter wonderland at Rise Hill. The southbound 'Waverley', headed by Gresley Class A3 Pacific No.60073 *St Gatien,* has just emerged from Rise Hill tunnel, hidden by smoke in the background, and approaches Dent station past a wall of compacted snow on 26th January 1963. The winter of 1962/63 was one of the harshest in living memory and the S&C line was particularly badly affected. On the night of 19th January the 10.05pm Edinburgh (Waverley) to St Pancras ran into snowdrifts near Dent during a blizzard and eventually returned to Carlisle, from where it continued to London via the East Coast Main Line. The S&C route was blocked for the next five days and through services diverted to run via Ingleton and the West Coast Main Line (WCML). Some remarkable sights resulted, such as Class A3 No.60082 *Neil Gow* working the 'Waverley' on 21st January and, even more unlikely, Class V2 2-6-2 No.60802 which was provided to haul the southbound 'Thames-Clyde Express' from Carlisle three days later. One wonders how many V2s have appeared on the WCML at the head of a named express. Later, further deep snowdrifts on the S&C line apparently defied all attempts at clearance and the route was out of action for long periods during March due to blockages between Mallerstang and Dent with through trains being once again diverted via Ingleton, although it is not clear whether any further incursions were made by Gresley V2s! One major casualty of the dislocated timetable was the London to Edinburgh (and vice versa) 'Waverley' which was suspended between Leeds and Carlisle for long periods. Congratulations to the photographer for braving the conditions and taking such a remarkable picture. *Gavin Morrison*

2nd · SINGLE    SINGLE · 2nd
Garsdale to
Garsdale            Garsdale
Dent              Dent
DENT
(M)     Fare    (M)
For conditions see over   For conditions see over

A southbound goods train, with BR Standard 'Britannia' Class Pacific No.70045 *Lord Rowallan* in charge, runs through Garsdale station on an overcast 10th August 1966. Besides being famous for the highest water troughs in the world, located on a rare section of level track just south of the station, Garsdale was also, in times past, the junction for the branch to Hawes. The contract for construction of the Hawes branch was not let until 1871 and the line's opening was delayed until the main line had been completed; Garsdale station was known as 'Hawes Junction' until 1932. Traffic was always sparse on the branch and the section beyond Hawes to Northallerton was closed to passengers from 26th April 1954 while services between Garsdale and Hawes survived until 16th March 1959. Another feature of Garsdale, in addition to the troughs, was the stockaded turntable, just north of the station on the down side, and there are stories of locomotives being blown around by high winds. Garsdale, the only junction station along the 72 miles-long S&C line, was intended to be a sizeable railway community and the MR had ambitious plans for 30 cottages and a locomotive shed capable of housing up to 30 locomotives, but at some point their grandiose ideas were considerably scaled down although some cottages were built on the down side and a small engine shed provided. The best-known building at Garsdale was probably the water tank house where the room underneath the tank had a small stage and piano and became the venue for social gatherings; the room is believed to have been converted and decorated for use as a 'village hall' some time after the First World War. Gatherings of an altogether different character took place in the down platform waiting room which was used for church services once a month. The MR had an aversion to facing points on the main line and trains from the south requiring access to the Hawes branch had to set back over a trailing crossover to access the outermost face of Garsdale station's island platform – a most peculiar arrangement. *Tommy Tomalin*

A good day at Garsdale. The 9.20am Manchester (Victoria) to Glasgow (Central) train steams through Garsdale behind rebuilt 'Patriot' No.45531 *Sir Frederick Harrison* on 3rd August 1963. This was one of those particularly interesting workings that made the study of railways so fascinating at that time because it was routed via Blackburn and then over the superb Settle and Carlisle line to Carlisle. It was then booked to travel over Beattock summit to Glasgow where the advertised arrival time was 3.35pm, only 35 minutes later than the regular 9.30am from Manchester which went via the West Coast Main Line. *Noel Machell*

Later, the photographer was rewarded by the sight of Peppercorn-designed Class A1 Pacific No.60146 *Peregrine* on the 6.35am Birmingham (New Street) to Glasgow (St Enoch) at the same location. North of Carlisle, this train travelled by the traditional route (via Dumfries) used by expresses on the Midland route to Carlisle and was due in Glasgow at 3.58pm. No.60146 was not the only member of its class operating on the Settle and Carlisle line that day because the photographer later saw No.60134 *Foxhunter* but his picture was ruined by the hazy conditions. Photography on that line has, in the author's experience, always been a very frustrating business, the main 'enemies' being never-ending horizontal rain in the winter and poor visibility due to haze in the summer. But when the sun does shine the landscape is absolutely breathtaking...... *Noel Machell*

THE SETTLE & CARLISLE LINE

A northbound goods working, with Stanier Class 5MT 4-6-0 No.45045 in charge, crosses Moorcock viaduct on 25th April 1966. Compared to other, more impressive civil engineering works on the S&C line, Moorcock viaduct may look rather insignificant but it presented the engineers building the line with one of their greatest challenges. An embankment was planned originally and earth was deposited into the moss which, even after four months of continuous tipping, simply swallowed up everything the navvies could throw at it – utter frustration! Eventually, in 1871 the seat of the embankment was drained and a trench cut into the peat in an effort to locate solid ground for the foundation of a viaduct. The 12-arch, 227 yards-long structure that eventually appeared was built on a curve and its fourth and eighth piers were strengthened. *Ron Herbert*

Notorious for its endless rain and buffeting winds that often rendered any kind of photography out of the question, here is incontrovertible proof that the sun did shine occasionally at Ais Gill. Pictured on a perfect evening with not a cloud to be seen, BR Standard Class 9F 2-10-0 No.92118 approaches Ais Gill signal box with a northbound goods on 17th April 1967. The fickle climate in this part of the world is legendary and it is possible that within a few minutes after this shot was taken the clouds rolled in from the west and deposited a deluge. *Ron Herbert*

The distinctive outline of Wild Boar fell (Great Britain's most photographed mountain?) looms over Stanier Class 8F 2-8-0 No.48304 as it makes a confident ascent to Ais Gill summit on an August afternoon in 1967. The summit signal box, which was brought into use on 26th April 1890, was the highest structure on the S&C line; it was closed on 28th January 1981 and later dismantled piece by piece for preservation. The box was connected to the road by a wooden walkway from the rear onto the embankment. Ais Gill signal box apparently did not have the luxury of piped water which was supplied on a daily basis by train and those with a sense of humour have commented that, ironically, it probably had more 'water' outside than any other signal box in Great Britain! What a pity this valuable natural resource was wasted. *Author*

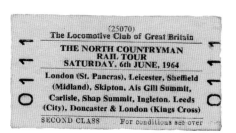

(25070)
The Locomotive Club of Great Britain

THE NORTH COUNTRYMAN
RAIL TOUR
SATURDAY, 6th JUNE, 1964

London (St. Pancras), Leicester, Sheffield (Midland), Skipton, Ais Gill Summit, Carlisle, Shap Summit, Ingleton, Leeds (City), Doncaster & London (Kings Cross)

SECOND CLASS      For conditions see over

The classic Ais Gill scene: wild, desolate but stunningly beautiful. The bare moorland stretches in all directions and Ais Gill Moor cottages, the only habitation in the immediate area, are just visible on the extreme right of the picture. The line of trees in the middle of the shot marks the course of Hell Gill beck, one of the sources of the river Eden which the railway follows for much of the way to Carlisle. This area is one of the principal watersheds of the Pennine range and, in addition to the river Eden, the Clough and Ure rivers have their sources within yards of each other on Lunds fell. The locomotive depicted, working a down freight train, is Stanier Class 8F No.48773 which is of special interest, not only because of its history but also due to it being the only member of its class to carry a diagonal yellow stripe on its cabsides; the stripes were, of course, applied in error but BR management were obsessed by diesel traction at the time and nobody bothered to have them painted over. No.48773 is undoubtedly the most widely travelled, and has the most colourful history, of any locomotive depicted in this book. Built in Glasgow by the North British Locomotive Co. in 1940 it operated with the LMSR (as No.8233) before being transferred to the War Department the following year as No.WD 307. It was shipped overseas and ran on the Iranian State Railway as No.41-109, but was repatriated in 1952, becoming No.WD 70307. After overhaul at Derby it was transferred to the Longmoor Military Railway and underwent yet another change of identity, being renumbered WD 500; it also worked for a time at Bicester. It was purchased by BR in 1957 and was initially allocated number 90733, apparently because somebody in the BR hierarchy had mistaken it for a WD Class 2-8-0! Running as No.48773 it operated in BR service for only a brief period until withdrawn by the Scottish Region in December 1962 during a massive purge of BR steam power prior to the formation of the British Railways Board. Its incredible career continued, however, and it was later reinstated by the London Midland Region, surviving right until the end of BR steam. It was later acquired for private preservation and, at the time of writing, No.48773 is based on the Severn Valley Railway. *Alan Reeve*

A pall of black smoke erupts skywards as an unknown 'Black Five' takes a long goods train through Mallerstang dale and attacks the last mile of the unrelenting 1 in 100 incline to Ais Gill summit. In the past enginemen probably suffered many anxious moments as they tackled the last stage of the climb from Ormside, particularly if their engine was in poor condition, but in this case the locomotive is 'blowing off' slightly so at least it was not short of steam. Hangman's bridge, which carried a farm track across the line, was located close to this spot; the bridge took its name from the gruesome act of a platelayer who supposedly committed suicide by hanging himself from the parapet. One of the glories of the S&C line is the manner in which the line is carried high up on the hillsides offering fine views of the landscape unobtainable from any road. The section of line through Mallerstang is no exception and is carried on a ledge above the valley and largely inaccessible but, remarkably, there was a signal box located in the dale, the signalman being obliged to trudge across fields to reach it – hardly an inviting prospect on a wet, windswept Pennine night. It must have been quite a climb, and when the post was advertised perhaps the job specification mentioned that applicants needed to be physically fit and mentally conditioned to tolerate working alone in such an isolated spot with, perhaps, a crackly telephone line to adjacent boxes as the only contact with the outside world. Birkett tunnel is located in the dale and was the site of an alarming rock fall when it was being excavated in the early 1870s. In addition to a workable vein of lead, limestone, grit, coal, slate and iron were also discovered prompting Mr John Crossley, the engineer-in-charge, to comment that it is 'the most curious combination I have ever seen'. *Alan Reeve*

Prior to closures that occurred in the early 1970s, the 9¾ miles-long stretch of line between Garsdale and Kirkby Stephen was the longest between stations, although in 1884 a station was almost built at Mallerstang but the MR asked local residents to fund the access road and the plan came to nought. Kirkby Stephen station was the large type of building characteristic of the MR at its best, perhaps the most attractive and distinctive features being the bargeboards and decorative glass waiting room screen visible in the middle of the picture. When this shot of Class 8F No.48313 passing through was taken on 7th August 1967 the premises had been partially commandeered by the civil engineer's department who had erected the rather unsightly porch visible towards the far end of the building. This protected the entrance to what was originally a first class waiting room and Kirkby Stephen station was the only one on the line to boast the undoubted luxury of this facility. The premises underwent various name changes during their lifetime, being known as 'Kirkby Stephen and Ravenstonedale' from 1900 only to revert to their original name in 1935. In 1953 the former LNER station in the town became known as 'Kirkby Stephen East' so the station on the S&C line was suffixed 'West'; the suffix was dropped in 1968, two years before the station was closed to passengers in May 1970. A small railway community developed around the station, including a rather grand house for the stationmaster and a row of more modest houses called 'Midland Terrace' while there are also a number of (even more modest!) single-storey cottages for workers known appropriately as 'Midland Cottages'. The station was re-opened in 1986 and is currently maintained in fine condition. *Tommy Tomalin*

A scene recorded at the south end of Appleby West station in the mid-1960s showing Stanier Class 5MT No.44884 taking water; the engine is 'blowing off' and the fireman has obviously been hard at work building up the fire for the task ahead. Note that the locomotive is fitted with a snowplough. Appleby station is, arguably, the most important intermediate station on the S&C line and has the distinction of being the only one originally provided with a footbridge which is partially visible in the picture. Part of the main station building can be seen on the left of the photograph while a section of the waiting shelter on the up platform is also visible. The ten-wagon cattle dock is in the foreground whilst on the right can be seen part of the substantially constructed water tank. Latterly, there were two signal boxes at Appleby, the one south of the station on the up side, which dated from 1890, being known as 'Appleby West'; this box closed on 14th October 1973. The other signal box, 'Appleby North' is also on the up side and replaced another nearby box that was destroyed by fire in 1951. Appleby station, like that at Kirkby Stephen, has undergone changes of identity over the years and was known as 'Appleby West' from 1952 to May 1968 to avoid confusion with the neighbouring Appleby East station on the Penrith to Barnard Castle route. There was a goods connection between the two lines and, latterly, this was used to access an army depot at Warcop following the closure of the former LNER route. A very sad chapter in the history of the station occurred on 13th May 1978 when one of Great Britain's most eminent railway photographers, Bishop Eric Treacy, collapsed and died on the station when waiting to photograph a steam rail tour. There is a plaque on the down platform commemorating this tragic event. *RCTS Photo Archive*

Pictured in glorious evening sunshine after a shower of rain, Stanier Class 5MT No.45364 is seen pulling away from Appleby with a local train from Hellifield to Carlisle; note that the coaches are in carmine and cream livery. This vintage photograph was taken on 6th September 1954. At the time of this picture BR was still suffering from the ravages of war-time neglect – note that the engine's top feed casing is missing. *Neil Davenport*

A northbound train hauled by Stanier 'Jubilee' Class 6P5F 4-6-0 No.45562 *Alberta* passes Culgaith some time in the early 1960s; note the LNER-designed rolling stock. *Alberta* was allocated to Holbeck shed (Leeds) for many years and had probably been a regular sight on the S&C line but it rose to fame in 1967 when it became one of the very last 'Jubilees' in BR traffic. No.45562 was one of a small number of these machines maintained in exemplary condition for working summer Saturday extra trains over the S&C line which attracted many lineside observers in addition to large contingents of enthusiasts who travelled on the trains. It is often said that all of the stations on the line were built to the same design but Culgaith, which is unfortunately hidden by smoke in this picture, was an exception. It was a late arrival on the scene and built at the suggestion of the local vicar and several landowners who wrote to MR headquarters at Derby requesting a station. The MR viewed the request favourably but insisted that a track must be laid from the village (located on a hill on the left of the picture) to the station. The premises opened on 1st April 1880 and a level crossing plus crossing keeper's house were provided and, of course, a signal box but that was replaced in 1908. Most unusually for the S&C line the platforms were mainly built of wood as was the waiting shelter on the down side, so Culgaith station has always been something of a curiosity. *RCTS Photo Archive*

BR Standard Class 9F 2-10-0 No.92161 bursts out of Culgaith tunnel at the head of a southbound goods working; this portrait is thought to have been taken in 1963. Note the lineside sign bearing the number 276 which could easily be mistaken as an indication of the mileage from London St Pancras. Actually, the sign denotes the number of the tunnel, while the distance from St Pancras at this point is, rather confusingly, just over 285 miles. Culgaith tunnel, 661 yards long, was cut through red marl and was constructed between 1871 and 1873. Remarkably for the S&C line there is a length of level track between Culgaith and Waste Bank tunnels, the longest on the entire route. *RCTS Photo Archive*

In this illustration, thought to have been taken in 1965, a morning Carlisle to Hellifield stopping train, with Stanier Class 5MT No.45259 in command, is depicted passing the sidings at Long Meg, between Little Salkeld and Lazonby. The modest load of three LMSR coaches and two vans is unlikely to have unduly taxed the locomotive. There was a mine here and the anhydrite produced was transported southwards to Widnes, the heavy trains always ensuring that the locomotive would invariably be working to its limit on the long climb up to Ais Gill. The mine's history can be traced back to 1896 when the Long Meg Plaster & Mineral Co. Ltd first developed its workings and movements by rail are thought to have commenced at that time. Regrettably, the workings were closed in the mid-1970s, thus robbing the S&C line of one of its few sources of originating traffic. Photographers were always attracted to the section of the S&C line south of Kirkby Stephen and interesting locations such as Long Meg seem to have been overlooked, so the author was especially pleased to obtain this view. *RCTS Photo Archive*

A further picture at Long Meg sidings, taken from a different angle, showing a morning train heading for Carlisle in 1965. Unfortunately, the identity of the train is uncertain but reference to the public timetable for that period indicates that it was probably the 7.34am Appleby West to Carlisle 'all stations' train; motive power is Ivatt Class 4MT 2-6-0 No.43049. The signal box at Long Meg was one of the more modern on the line, dating from 3rd July 1955 when it replaced a much older structure; it was closed in 1983 but had a brief reprieve being temporarily reopened on 17th November 1983 following a mishap on the West Coast Main Line. Note the two platelayers walking on the track, one of whom must have stepped back onto the track immediately after the train had passed. The river Eden is just out of sight on the right of the picture and, indeed, the railway crosses the river on Eden Lacy viaduct a few hundred yards north of this point. *RCTS Photo Archive*

There was a purely local service for work people that ran between Appleby West and Carlisle (and vice versa) consisting of a morning train which, in the winter 1964/65 timetable, left Appleby at 7.34am and returned from the border city at 6.05pm, arriving in Appleby at 7.04pm; on Saturdays the return working left Carlisle an hour later. These trains provided the rare opportunity to photograph tank locomotives on the S&C line and in this portrait Fowler-designed Class 4MT 2-6-4T No.42369 is seen setting off from its Armathwaite station stop in the evening sunshine with the 6.05pm *ex*-Carlisle on 21st May 1963. The operation of these trains presumably involved a lot of costly 'light engine' running to and from Carlisle and it is, perhaps, surprising that they were still steam worked at this time. *Bob Leslie/ Peter Robinson collection*

Towards the end of their lives the 'Royal Scot' Class 7P locomotives could be found on quite menial work and the glory days are clearly over for No.46140 *The King's Royal Rifle Corps* which was photographed coasting to its Armathwaite station stop; it was powering the three-coach 4.37pm Carlisle to Bradford (Forster Square) local train on 1st June 1963. During its career No.46140 had been allocated to Crewe (North), Kentish Town, Longsight and Newton Heath sheds so it was a widely travelled machine; it survived to become one of the last operational members of its class. Part of the main station building can be seen on the left of the shot and in more prosperous times the structure accommodated a large stationmaster's office, general waiting room, ladies waiting room, porters' room and lamp room; there were also the usual lavatory facilities. There was a small goods yard with a cattle dock and substantial goods shed on the down side of the line, north of the station; goods facilities were withdrawn from 6th April 1964. Armathwaite's lofty signal box, brought into use on 16th July 1899, is of wooden construction and can just be discerned beyond the last coach of the train; it was closed on 15th January 1983. *Bob Leslie/Peter Robinson collection*

A Class 4F 0-6-0, No.44277, plods slowly uphill near Cotehill with the daily Carlisle to Skipton 'pick up' goods working on 22nd December 1962. A gradient of 1 in 132 applies at this spot, but the crew would have been aware that there was a short respite of 1 in 132 downhill after the site of Cotehill station had been passed. Alas, it was almost the last downhill stretch before Ais Gill! *Bob Leslie/Peter Robinson collection*

Another picture taken near Cotehill in cold and clear winter conditions – just right for photography. Here Stanier Class 5MT No.44677 takes a goods working from Durran Hill up the incline towards the site of Cotehill station and lays a splendid smoke effect across the Cumberland countryside; this picture was taken on 2nd February 1963. There were a number of variants of this class, most notably those engines fitted with Caprotti valve gear, and at the time of this photograph No.44677 was running with a self-weighing tender and small snowplough, making it a very distinctive machine in its own right. In times past there were two interesting industrial branches in this area, one of which diverged from the S&C line on the down side just before Cotehill station. That siding served Robinson's Knott Mill plaster works but the track was removed in 1940 and all trace has since disappeared. The other private siding originally served the brick and tile works of Mr Claude Lonsdale, who traded as the Carlisle Brick and Tile Company, and converged with the S&C line on the up side near the Howe & Co. sidings signal box. In 1943 new sidings were laid at this location to meet the requirements of the Ministry of Supply. *Bob Leslie/Peter Robinson collection*

The last vestiges of the winter snows lie on the grass by the side of the track as Stanier 'Black Five' No.44790 heads southwards with a mixed goods train between Duncowfold and Cotehill on 2nd April 1966. Note the sizeable permanent way hut on the left of the shot.
*Bob Leslie/Peter Robinson collection*

A total of 733 Class WD 2-8-0s came into BR ownership after the end of the Second World War so it would be reasonable to assume that they would be a regular sight on the S&C line, particularly as so many were based in the West Riding of Yorkshire. They were, however, infrequent visitors and this is the only 'publishable' shot of one of these machines on the route. Here, No.90533 is seen ambling along with a Carlisle to Skipton goods near Cumwhinton on 1st June 1963. Constructed by Vulcan Foundry in June 1943, No.90533 ran as War Department No.77062 for some years and entered BR stock in December 1948; it was based on the Southern Region at Bricklayer's Arms shed in the very early 1950s. Later in its career No.90533 moved to Newton Heath shed, Manchester, and appears to have spent the rest of its working life at that shed, being withdrawn in February 1966. *Bob Leslie/ Peter Robinson collection*

Photographed on a lovely summer day, Hughes/Fowler Class 6P5F 2-6-0 No.42790, powering a Durran Hill to Stourton goods train, works hard on the 1 in 132 gradient through Cumwhinton station; this picture was taken on 16th July 1955. Note that the three vehicles immediately behind the locomotive are cattle wagons which, like the rest of the short-wheelbase vehicles forming the train, have long since been consigned to history. The trailing crossover, which gave access to the goods yard, was a characteristic feature of the S&C line, as previously mentioned. The neat and tidy condition of the station is also noteworthy and, presumably, the gentleman walking along the platform was one of the very few staff employed at Cumwhinton station which was situated only about five miles from Carlisle and unlikely to have been busy; judging by the attractive flower beds at least one member of staff was a dedicated gardener. The signal box dated from 1897 and remained in use until 1st March 1958. The railway authorities thoughtfully displayed a Ribble bus timetable, next to the former LMSR notice board, and this would have been essential reading for any passengers unlucky enough to miss their last train home. A substantially-built, and quite commodious, three-bedroom stationmaster's house was provided in addition to a row of four cottages for employees. Sadly, the relaxed and unhurried way of life at Cumwhinton could not last forever and the station was closed from 5th November 1956. *Bob Leslie/Peter Robinson collection*

The Glasgow-bound 'Thames-Clyde Express' is seen standing in the unmistakable surroundings of Carlisle station on 20th August 1960. The photographer had just experienced an exhilarating run on the footplate of Class A3 No.60082 *Neil Gow* which had recouped around 18 minutes on the schedule, following a late start from Leeds. What a creditable performance and one, no doubt, the photographer thoroughly enjoyed. *Gavin Morrison*

Clapham Junction, in south London, is probably one of the best-known stations in Great Britain but here, for a change, is a picture of the 'other' Clapham Junction, in North Yorkshire. It may not have quite such an intensive service but at least the scenery is far better, even on the kind of dreary day depicted in this photograph. A Hughes/Fowler Class 6P5F 2-6-0, No.42851, rounds the curve from the Carnforth direction with an unidentified train on 28th July 1962. The tracks going straight ahead are those to Ingleton and Low Gill, where they joined the West Coast Main Line. This line was built in stages, the first section as far as Ingleton being opened in 1849 by the North Western Railway while the stretch on to Low Gill was brought into use by the LNWR in 1861. The principal intermediate place served by this route was the small town of Ingleton so it was probably not surprising that the line lost its local passenger service from 1st February 1954. It remained open to goods traffic, however, and its usefulness as a diversionary route certainly became apparent in early 1963, when the Settle and Carlisle line was blocked by snow for weeks on end and expresses from St Pancras to Scotland ran via Ingleton. Sadly, the line was later closed completely and the track was removed in the mid-1960s. The line to Carnforth was also constructed in stages, the section from Clapham Junction to Wennington (and on to Lancaster) coming into use on 1st June 1850, while the gap between Wennington and Carnforth was bridged by the Furness and Midland Joint line that opened in 1867. *John Langford*

On 10th May 1965 the gantry carrying the Southern Region's Clapham Junction 'A' signal box across the tracks partially collapsed, causing total dislocation of services to and from Waterloo station. The civil engineer responsible for the Settle Junction to Carnforth line, mindful of events in the capital, had clearly decreed that 'his' Clapham Junction signal box should be encased in baulks of timber in order to support the fragile structure and avoid an embarrassing repetition. It may not look pretty but at least the box was still in one piece when this picture was taken in June 1968. *Author*

Following the opening of the link to Carnforth in 1867, Wennington station became a relatively busy country junction because trains from the West Riding to Carnforth/Morecambe were divided there and those in the opposite direction combined. These procedures are easy with multiple unit trains but much less so with ordinary coaching stock and, of course, separate locomotives would have been needed for each portion. In this picture 'Black Five' No.44894 is seen leaving Wennington with the 1.53pm from Leeds (City) on 6th March 1965 while a diesel unit waits for the 'road' on the other track. The local stations between Wennington and Carnforth had been closed by this date; Melling was shut from 5th May 1952 while Arkholme and Borwick lasted until 12th September 1960. Wennington lost its status as a junction station when the line to Lancaster was closed from 3rd January 1966 and henceforth Lancaster and Morecambe passengers were obliged to travel via Carnforth. *Noel Machell*

The two-coach 12.20pm Carnforth to Leeds (City) train, with Fairburn Class 4MT 2-6-4T No.42198 in charge, heads towards Wennington near Over Kellet on 19th May 1964. On arrival at Wennington this train would eventually have been coupled to the 12.30pm *ex*-Morecambe (Promenade), and the winter 1964/65 timetable indicates that the Carnforth portion spent no less than 28 minutes at Wennington before departing at 1.06pm. It should be mentioned, however, that another train was timed to accomplish the 'attachment' in only ten minutes. The long wait endured by passengers aboard the 12.20pm from Carnforth did at least provide the opportunity for a visit to the local hostelry for a quick beer and a sandwich! *Noel Machell*

When viewed from the rear even their best friends would not describe the Fowler Class 4MT 2-6-4Ts as handsome and here No.42301 is pictured leaving Carnforth with the 7.00pm Leeds train on 3rd July 1964. The train is leaving from a former 'Midland' bay platform while the tracks on the right of the photograph are those serving the Barrow line platforms. In times past the Barrow line platforms were covered by an overall roof but this feature is understood to have been swept away by the LMSR in the 1930s when the station was modernised. *Noel Machell*

Fierce gradients, breathtaking moorland scenery and impressive, lofty viaducts: the route between Penrith/Tebay and Darlington via Barnard Castle was undoubtedly one of the most spectacular in Great Britain. The line to Tebay was constructed primarily to convey coke from the Durham area to the iron and steel industry's blast furnaces around Barrow-in-Furness/Workington and transport ore in the opposite direction. The trains were routed from Tebay along the main west coast line to Hincaster Junction and then on to Barrow via Arnside. A meeting to promote the line took place in Kirkby Stephen on 18th November 1856 and the South Durham & Lancashire Union Railway received the Royal Assent on 13th July 1857, the capital originally authorised to build the line being £553,000. The first mineral trains ran between Tebay and Barnard Castle on 4th July 1861 while the formal opening took place on 7th August. The inaugural passenger trains ran the following day, thus enabling ordinary folk to admire the fabulous scenery and marvel at the magnificent civil engineering work necessary in order to cross the natural barrier of the high Pennines. A line northwards from Kirkby Stephen to Penrith (Eden Valley Junction) was also proposed and obtained enthusiastic support from local landowners and the Eden Valley Railway received the Royal Assent on 21st May 1858 (note the history of that line is covered in the next section). In this picture BR Standard Class 4MT No.76050 exerts maximum effort soon after leaving Tebay with a Blackpool to Darlington train on 1st August 1959. The train is formed of six coaches of both Gresley and Thompson-designed stock. *Bob Leslie/Peter Robinson collection*

The 11.20am Blackpool to Newcastle-upon-Tyne train is depicted soon after departure from Tebay on 1st August 1959; motive power is provided by two BR Standard 2-6-0s, Class 3MT No.77002 piloting Class 4MT No.76024. The West Coast Main Line can just be discerned in the distance on the right of the picture, its course being marked by telegraph poles and a small permanent way cabin. The Tebay to Kirkby Stephen section of line lost its regular passenger trains as far back as 1st December 1952 so it was quite an early closure, long before Doctor Beeching stalked the corridors of No.222 Marylebone Road. The route was not closed completely, however, and remained open for goods and seasonal passenger trains between the north-east of England and Lancashire resorts, principally Blackpool. In addition it was used by unadvertised special workings conveying miners to places such as Grange-over-Sands to convalesce so it still saw a fair amount of traffic. *Bob Leslie/Peter Robinson collection*

The line that 'closed' twice. The Tebay to Kirkby Stephen section had a curious claim to fame because two 'last' trains traversed that stretch of line, the original one being an evening service from Tebay to Kirkby Stephen on 30th November 1952 hauled by Ivatt Class 2MT 2-6-0 No.46480. That 'last' passenger working merely commemorated the withdrawal of the regular local service and not complete closure of the line which continued to be regularly used by goods and summer passenger trains, as previously mentioned. The second 'last' train marked the complete closure of the Barnard Castle to Penrith route, including the line down to Tebay, and that was a rail tour promoted by the Railway Correspondence & Travel Society which started at Darlington and traversed the entire Stainmore route on 20th January 1962. This train was powered by a pair of BR Standard 2-6-0s, Class 3MT No.77003 and Class 4MT No.76049, and in this portrait the fireman of train engine No.76049 prepares to relinquish the single line tablet to the Ravenstonedale signalman for the very last time. The section of line from Tebay to Ravenstonedale was double track but only single from Ravenstonedale on to the junction at Kirkby Stephen. *Gavin Morrison*

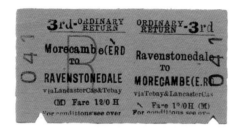

The summit at Stainmore has given its name to the route but there is another demanding climb between Ravenstonedale and Kirkby Stephen up to Sandy Bank summit (889 feet above sea level). Compared to Stainmore, the little-known Sandy Bank summit was relatively minor but, even so, was only 28 feet lower than Shap! In this picture Ivatt Class 4MT 2-6-0 No.43072, hauling the 11.05am Blackpool to Darlington train on 17th August 1957, is depicted coasting down from the summit across Smardale Gill viaduct. *Bob Leslie/Peter Robinson collection*

Few railway structures are located in such a beautiful and dramatic setting as the graceful Smardale Gill viaduct which blends so perfectly with its surroundings; the 14-arch viaduct is 553 feet long. The tumbling waters of Scandal Beck can be seen in the foreground while in the background the slopes of Crosby Garrett fell form the backdrop. Here, the 9.20am Darlington to Blackpool train, headed by Ivatt Class 4MT 2-6-0 No.43050, crosses the viaduct on 3rd August 1957. Smardale Gill viaduct should not be confused with another viaduct of a similar name on the Settle and Carlisle line which passes over the Tebay to Kirkby Stephen route a mile or so east of this point. *Bob Leslie/Peter Robinson collection*

The Stainmore route is famous for its long stretches built across bleak, open moorland as the line traverses the high North Pennines but, in complete contrast, around Smardale it is surrounded by trees as it runs along a ledge above Scandal Beck. In this shot Ivatt Class 4MT 2-6-0 No.43072 disturbs the tranquillity of the gill near Smardale as it heads westwards with the 7.32am South Shields to Blackpool train on 3rd August 1957. Holiday-makers looking forward to their well-earned fortnight's break by the sea were presumably undeterred by the very early departure time from South Shields. In the summer 1960 timetable three summer Saturday holiday trains, from Darlington, Newcastle-upon-Tyne and South Shields, and their corresponding return workings, were advertised over the Stainmore route though it is likely others would have been provided by BR if the demand warranted extra trains. *Bob Leslie/ Peter Robinson collection*

Many thousands of colour photographs of trains crossing Smardale viaduct on the Settle and Carlisle line, in the background, must have been taken over the years but this is the only colour picture of a train passing the former Smardale station the author has ever seen. This view shows BR Standard Class 3MT 2-6-0 No.77001 passing through with an eastbound train of empty wagons on 4th September 1954. The Tebay to Kirkby Stephen line passed under the southernmost arch of Smardale viaduct so two of the most spectacular routes in Great Britain were in very close proximity, albeit for a very short distance. Smardale was the scene of a nasty accident on 20th May 1955 when two class Q6 locomotives were derailed when working tender-first on a train bound for Kirkby Stephen; the incident was attributed to a combination of track that had not been secured following repair work and a broken tender spring on one of the locomotives. The Q6s had apparently been transferred to Kirkby Stephen temporarily but following this incident the class was banished from the line, never to reappear in normal traffic. The tiny station of Smardale Halt was, unfortunately, partially situated under a roadbridge but this did not prevent it carrying off a prize for the best kept station garden competition in the 1930s. The halt did not, apparently, issue tickets and the staff had to arrange for them to be provided at the next station down the line! Smardale Halt lost both its passenger and goods facilities from 1st December 1952. *Neil Davenport*

In the 1840s various fanciful schemes were put forward for trans-Pennine routes including a proposal by the Yorkshire and Glasgow Union Railway for a line from Thirsk through Wensleydale to Hawes. The route would then have been along the Mallerstang valley to Kirkby Stephen from where it would have reached Clifton, on the Lancaster and Carlisle line, via Appleby. Needless to say this scheme never came to fruition. In the 1850s a more realistic proposal was made by the Eden Valley Railway to construct a line from Kirkby Stephen along the upper valley of the river Eden to Clifton and the Act of Parliament authorising this scheme was passed on 21st May 1858. The symbolic cutting of the first sod took place at Appleby on 28th July 1858, the ceremony being performed by Lord Brougham. This event was followed by a procession through the town and a grand dinner in a tent that had been erected behind the King's Head Hotel; later there was a ball so it can be assumed that the townspeople welcomed the coming of the railway. Construction of the 22 miles-long route across low lying land was in the hands of Lawton Brothers of Newcastle and the task was relatively easy compared to the building of the nearby line over Stainmore summit; building the line reputedly cost £204,803. There were seven intermediate stations, by far the most important being that serving Appleby, although its position above the town was not particularly convenient. The line opened for mineral traffic on 8th April 1862 while the first passenger trains ran two months later. The relatively flat Kirkby Stephen to Penrith (Clifton) route lacked the drama of the Stainmore line and, in view of the paucity of pictures submitted for this book, it seems it was not a favourite with railway photographers. Here, BR Standard Class 3MT No.82027 has just taken the Appleby line at Eden Valley Junction with a train from Penrith to Darlington on 6th August 1956. Rather strangely, the Appleby branch appears to go straight ahead from the junction while the West Coast Main Line is on quite a tight curve. Note also the composition of the train which is made up of three brake coaches so passenger accommodation would have been rather restricted, but at least the guard would have been able to choose his carriage!
*Bob Leslie/Peter Robinson collection*

A delightful pastoral scene just east of Clifton Moor station on 21st May 1956 as BR Standard Class 3MT 2-6-2T No.82027 eases away from its station stop with the 2.57pm Penrith to Darlington train. On the left of the picture a group of people are enjoying a picnic by the side of the track and their dog seems to be showing considerable interest in the passing train. Clifton Moor station can just be discerned in the background beyond the roadbridge. The village of Clifton was once served by two stations, the other being Clifton and Lowther on the main line, but that lost its passenger service as long ago as 4th July 1938. *Bob Leslie/Peter Robinson collection*

| 2nd · SINGLE | | SINGLE · 2nd |
|---|---|---|
| | Clifton Moor To | |
| Clifton Moor Penrith | | Clifton Moor Penrith |
| | **PENRITH** | |
| (M) 0/9 | Fare | 0/9 (M) |
| For conditions see over | | For conditions see over |

0599 0599

Many thousands of photographs must have been taken at the former Appleby West station, on the Settle and Carlisle line, over the years but here, for a change, is a picture of Appleby East. This really vintage scene depicts Class J21 0-6-0 No.65103 entering the station with a Penrith to Darlington train on 7th September 1954. Note the bicycle leaning against the wall of the signal box: presumably the signalman lived locally! The station here, as previously mentioned, was remote from the centre of the town – note the fields in the background – and this could not have helped to foster traffic. Some of the stations between Kirkby Stephen and Penrith served only very small settlements and were earmarked for closure in the early 1950s. Musgrave lost its goods facilities from 3rd November 1952, the passenger service following on 1st December of the same year. Passenger trains ceased to call at Kirkby Thore and Temple Sowerby from 7th December 1953, while Cliburn lasted until 17th September 1956, so when closure came the only intermediate stations open for business were Warcop, Appleby East and Clifton. *Neil Davenport*

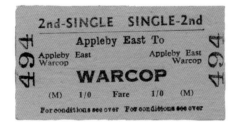

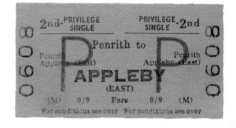

A view of the sizeable and elegant station building of Appleby East is seen in this illustration which dates from 23rd April 1960; the building was constructed in 1861 so was almost 100 years old at the time of this picture. The short section of line between Appleby Junction signal box, where the connection from the Settle and Carlisle line converged, and Appleby East station was double track. When the Stainmore line was closed certain sections remained open for goods and military traffic, the most important being the link from Appleby to Merrygill quarry which also served the Warcop army base. This section was truncated from 31st October 1974 when the Merrygill trains ceased to operate but traffic continued to Warcop and, indeed, very occasionally troop trains ran, usually hauled by Class 40 diesel locomotives. Access to the Warcop line was gained via a connection controlled by Appleby North signal box on the Settle and Carlisle line. The last recorded train along the branch to Warcop was a goods working on 16th March 1989. The short stub from Eden Valley Junction to Clifton Moor continued in use for goods traffic until 6th July 1964. *Stuart Ackley collection*

The end of the line. Bathed in glorious winter sunshine the Railway Correspondence and Travel Society's 'Stainmore Limited' rail tour stands at Kirkby Stephen East station on 20th January 1962. Both locomotives were BR Standard 2-6-0s, Class 3MT No.77003 and Class 4MT No.76049 and their shining paintwork presents a heart-warming sight, but one wonders if it really lifted the gloom and all-pervading sadness of the participants who were making their last journey over the breathtaking Stainmore route. Note the vintage signal, complete with its wooden post, and empty locomotive shed in the background. In times past the shed was probably a bustling little place, bearing in mind the number of trains over Stainmore summit requiring pilots or banking assistance, and in 1950 its allocation was a total of 11 0-6-0s of classes J21 and J25. By 1959, however, those veterans had been ousted by much more up-to-date BR Standard classes, the total allocation being the same. *Gavin Morrison*

An old timer returns. The Class J21 0-6-0s were associated with the Stainmore route for decades but were largely displaced when more modern Ivatt-designed Class 4MT 2-6-0s and BR Standard types were introduced in the 1950s. The North Eastern branch of the RCTS organised a tour using Class J21 No.65033 which gave enthusiasts a final opportunity to travel over this famous route behind one of these sturdy machines; the train is depicted here entering Kirkby Stephen East station on 7th May 1960. No.65033 first saw the light of day as long ago as March 1889 and it survived to be the final member of its class in traffic, not being taken out of service until April 1962. The first part of the journey was from Darlington to Tebay, from where the J21 made an unassisted climb to Shap summit in a very creditable 13½ minutes; the train later returned from Carlisle to Darlington via Penrith and Appleby East. Unfortunately, the train was over-subscribed and many intending passengers had to be turned away; if other J21s had still been available the RCTS would presumably have requested a double-header with more coaches to cater for the overflow! If only........... *Gavin Morrison*

An overall view of the track layout and signalling arrangements at the eastern end of Kirkby Stephen East station with J21 Class 0-6-0 No.65103 running into the station with a Darlington to Penrith train on 31st August 1954. The signal box, partially visible in the middle of the shot, is Kirkby Stephen East while the roadbridge beyond carries the B6259 road to Hawes which passes Ais Gill summit on the Settle and Carlisle line; it may not be apparent from the picture but between the signal box and bridge the line crosses the foaming waters of the river Eden. The distant fells, some of which rise to over 2,000 feet above sea level, are an awe-inspiring sight. *Neil Davenport*

*PENRITH TO BARNARD CASTLE*

The crew of a train to Darlington pose for the camera in the afternoon sunshine at Kirkby Stephen East station, also on 31st August 1954. It is interesting to note that the old order on the line was still represented by Class J21s, as seen in the previous picture, but it was being supplanted by the 'new order' in the shape of BR Standard locomotives such as Class 2MT 2-6-0 No.78019 which was only five months old at the time of the photograph. No.78019 had been out-shopped from Darlington works (appropriately!) in March of the same year. The station building is still in existence at the time of writing as the centrepiece of a small railway preservation centre. *Neil Davenport*

A six-coach Blackpool to South Shields train, powered by Ivatt Class 4MT 2-6-0 No.43015, crosses Belah viaduct on an overcast 18th July 1959. Construction of this fascinating structure nominally commenced on 25th November 1857 when the foundation stone was laid by Henry Pease of Darlington, vice chairman of the South Durham and Lancashire Union Railway and also a local member of parliament. Twenty months elapsed, however, before work really got underway on 19th July 1859, the contractors being Gilkes, Wilson & Company, who made very rapid progress with the construction, and it was stated that it took the contractors only 43 days to reach the central, eighth pier from the Barras end of the viaduct. No scaffolding was apparently needed during the building of the viaduct and, incredibly, not a single accident occurred during its construction, a very creditable achievement bearing in mind the dangers involved. The viaduct, which consisted of 15 wrought iron piers, was 1,047 feet long and a maximum of 196 feet above the valley floor; it carried the railway across the river Belah. One of the structure's particularly interesting features was the manner in which the ironwork tapered, being around 50 feet wide at the base but less than half of that at the top. The total cost of construction was £31,630, a trifling sum by today's values. A major event in the structure's more recent history was its complete repainting in 1956 and 'official' photographs were apparently taken to illustrate the transformation in its appearance. Railway staff often regarded the appearance of a BR painting team as a bad omen, suggesting that closure was looming, and the work was being undertaken to inflate the operating costs of a route being considered for closure. Such cynicism was certainly justified on the Stainmore route because just seven years after substantial expenditure on painting the viaduct, the demolition men moved in to dismantle the structure, the work commencing on 13th August 1963 when the first span was felled at the Kirkby Stephen end. A tragic end to an iconic railway viaduct. *Bob Leslie/Peter Robinson collection*

A view from the other side of Belah viaduct showing the 11.20am Blackpool (Central) to Newcastle-upon-Tyne train crossing with a brace of BR Standard 2-6-0s in charge, Class 2MT No.78016 and Class 4MT No.76024; this picture was also taken on 18th July 1959. The 8-coach formation is made up of a mix of BR Standard coaches plus LNER Gresley- and Thompson-designed vehicles. On the WCML this train called at Preston, Lancaster, Carnforth and Oxenholme, but a stop at Tebay, where an engine change was probably scheduled, was not shown in the public timetable perhaps because the section onwards to Kirkby Stephen was not open to regular, all-year-round passenger traffic. This meant that trains such as this 'disappeared' from the London Midland Region public timetable and then mysteriously turned up again at Kirkby Stephen East in the North Eastern Region timetable! This train was advertised to arrive in Newcastle-upon-Tyne at 5.07pm. Note Belah signal box, in the far distance on the other side of the line, where night duty in particular must have been very lonely, and at times a rather frightening experience during spells of violent Pennine weather. The great mass of Winton fell rises up to a maximum of 2,171 feet above sea level behind the viaduct. *Bob Leslie/Peter Robinson collection*

A rare colour portrait of a train standing in Barras station on 31st August 1954. Judging by the way the smoke and steam are blowing around, this shot seems to have been taken on a very windy day and in the author's experience calm days were very much the exception high up in the Pennines. The black smoke being emitted by the locomotive suggests that the fireman had just put some more coal on BR Standard Class 2MT No.78019's fire to maintain boiler pressure. A stop at windswept Barras station, which served just a few isolated cottages, at least gave enginemen the opportunity to raise steam for the rest of the 1 in 59 climb to Stainmore summit, about three miles distant. *Neil Davenport*

The lack of passenger facilities on the westbound platform at Barras station is apparent in this photograph which was taken on 24th April 1960. The eastbound platform boasted a larger building, partially visible on the left of the picture, which presumably contained some sort of modest booking office and waiting room. The amenities at Barras may not have been in the top bracket but this was compensated by the absolutely incomparable views of the surrounding fells. In the summer 1960 timetable the first train to Darlington was the 11.51am (arrival time 12.53pm) while the last train back left at 4.34pm, so it was debatable whether this provided sufficient time for lunch and an afternoon shopping expedition.
*Stuart Ackley collection*

A Blackpool to South Shields train, headed by rather dirty Ivatt-designed Class 4MT 2-6-0 No.43073, assaults the final stage of the climb to Stainmore summit on an overcast 2nd August 1958. This picture was taken at Bleath Gill (Bleak Gill!), a location immortalised in the classic film 'Snowdrift at Bleath Gill' which was produced by the British Transport Commission's film unit. The area around here was often affected by exceptionally heavy snowfalls, the winters of 1942, 1947 and 1955 being particularly harsh when the Kirkby Stephen to Darlington line was completely blocked by snow. Cuttings became unrecognisable due to being completely filled by snow while there are remarkable pictures of Barras station totally engulfed by massive drifts up to roof height. What an absolutely outstanding line this was! *Bob Leslie/Peter Robinson collection*

The prominent sign on the right of the picture certainly left passengers in no doubt that they had passed the summit of the line and would soon be speeding, well almost, down to Darlington. The summit signs are thought to have been installed by the LNER in the 1930s when they replaced wooden boards. Cottages were built to house Stainmore signalmen, these being located just west of the signal box. A signalman once said that he spent the happiest days of his life at the remote Stainmore box, witnessing the beauty of a sunrise on a summer morning and hearing the call of grouse in the heather. Even better was the occasional sighting of the brilliant Northern Lights, seen during a night shift. A BR Standard Class 4MT 2-6-0, No.76050, passes the summit marker sign with a summer Saturday working from Blackpool on 5th August 1961; note that the train is formed of LMSR-designed stock. *Gavin Morrison*

A further scene at Stainmore summit, this time on 18th August 1958, showing a goods working comprising an assortment of wagons of various shapes and sizes heading to West Auckland; the train engine is BR Standard Class 2MT No.78013 while the pilot is No.78017 of the same class. The photographer comments that No.78017 had banked the train from Kirkby Stephen and on arrival at the summit ran-round and continued as pilot, as seen here. One of the line's most interesting relics can still be seen high up on the fells; this is a reservoir specially dug to provide water to the facilities at the summit. A channel was cut, along which water flowed, and this is also believed to be extant. Note traffic on the adjoining A66 main road which ran parallel to the line all the way from near Bleath Gill to Bowes. *Gavin Morrison*

The stopping trains between Darlington and Penrith were usually worked by Metro-Cammell diesel multiple units which replaced steam trains from 3rd February 1958, but on 7th August 1961 BR Standard Class 4MT 2-6-0 No.76050 was rostered to work the 10.50am Darlington to Penrith train in place of the more usual diesel unit. Here, No.76050 is seen pausing at Bowes as a break in the clouds allows the sun to burst through; note the fair number of people milling about on the platform. The average journey time for diesel stopping trains between Darlington and Penrith was usually just under two hours and one suspects that the crew aboard No.76050 would have been very hard pressed to keep to the timings, particularly bearing in mind the need for water stops.
*Charles Firminger*

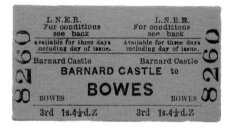

The photographer once again took advantage of a break in the cloud cover and recorded this scene at Bowes station on the same day. Bowes possessed a really fine, substantially constructed station building which was located on the Darlington-bound platform. Note the living accommodation for the stationmaster, and platform oil lamps; the signal box was located at the far end of that platform. Sadly, by the time of this photograph the once lovingly maintained gardens were running wild. The small goods yard, which consisted of just two roads, was on the westbound side of the line. The gradients on this part of the route were modest compared to elsewhere and westbound trains were faced with nothing more taxing than 1 in 93 for the next few miles, although the final climb to Stainmore summit was a more demanding 1 in 68.
*Charles Firminger*

The first railway to reach Barnard Castle was the Darlington and Barnard Castle Railway which opened on 9th July 1856 and terminated just north of the town centre. On 8th August 1861 the South Durham and Lancashire Union Railway opened for business and this served a separate station on the northern edge of the town. Through passengers had to walk between the two stations, a most inconvenient arrangement, and it was quickly decided that an enlarged through station serving both companies was preferable. This opened on 1st May 1862 from which date the first station in the town was closed but it remained in use for goods traffic and, ironically, survived in this guise until 5th April 1965, therefore just outlasting the premises that replaced it over a century earlier! The next landmark in the development of railways in the town was the construction of the route to West Auckland, this opening in August 1863. The 'second' station at Barnard Castle was an absolute gem with a character all of its own; it consisted of a single, curving through platform with bays at each end but the easternmost bay was taken out of use in around 1954. The central part of the platform was covered by a modest overall roof that had a canopy extension at the west end which dated from 1949. There were two signal boxes latterly, the east box controlling the level crossing at that end of the station in addition to a bank of sidings north of the station. In more prosperous times there was an engine shed at Barnard Castle, this being extant from 1864 to 1937, when it was closed. This illustration shows the station as it was on 7th August 1961; the west signal box can just be discerned beyond the trainshed in the middle of the picture. The old station was still in use for goods traffic at this time so this may explain the empty sidings. The doors of Barnard Castle station were closed for the final time on 28th November 1964 when the last trains ran on the Middleton-in-Teesdale branch. *Charles Firminger*

This splendid array of semaphore signals brightens up an otherwise dreary day at Barnard Castle station in the mid-1950s. It may not be immediately apparent, but the tracks to the old station ran behind the signal box while the engine shed was sited on the left of the main line beyond the level crossing. Note the two vintage horse boxes on the left. *Neil Davenport*

It is arguable whether a shot taken at Middleton-in-Teesdale qualifies for inclusion in this album but who could resist including this charming picture of immaculate, Gresley-designed Class V3 2-6-2T No.67636? The train depicted is the 10.00am from Middleton-in-Teesdale to Darlington and this picture was taken on 7th August 1961. Curiously, the station was situated in (what is now) North Yorkshire while the town was on the other side of the river Tees and, therefore, over the border in County Durham. In the early years of the 19th century Middleton-in-Teesdale had become a boom town due to the area's vast deposits of lead, and when the trans-Pennine route from Barnard Castle to Tebay was opened in 1861 there was unbridled optimism and thoughts turned to a link between Barnard Castle and Alston. Support for this ambitious scheme was disappointing, however, and the promoters were forced to consider the more realistic idea of a line between Barnard Castle and Middleton-in-Teesdale only which, they hoped, would still carry considerable mineral traffic. The 7½ miles-long branch was planned to diverge from the Stainmore route at Tees Valley Junction, just over a mile west of Barnard Castle, and three intermediate stations were envisaged. The necessary Act of Parliament was granted on 19th June 1865 and the first sod was ceremonially cut by the Duke of Cleveland at Middleton-in-Teesdale on 9th November 1865. The line took three years to complete and it is recorded that it was constructed by Mr Boulton, a local contractor, and the cost was £28,244 11s 6d. The summit of the line was 210 feet above sea level at Mickleton. The official opening took place on 12th May 1868 while public services commenced the following day. The discovery of high quality ironstone at Holwick, about three miles north of Middleton-in-Teesdale, prompted the construction of a tramway to the terminus and other quarries were directly connected to the goods yard. Originally, there was an engine shed at the terminus, but this was closed in 1959 and demolished two years later; a turntable was also provided until it was removed in the 1940s and the pit subsequently filled-in. The year 1951 marked the start of a gradual decline in the line's fortunes when one of the quarries on the line decided to switch to road transport and in 1954 the intermediate stations became unstaffed. In 1963 the inevitable announcement was made that BR was seeking to withdraw the passenger service and this took place, with little local opposition, in November 1964; goods traffic lingered until 5th April 1965. *Charles Firminger*

*THE MIDDLETON-IN-TEESDALE BRANCH*

In 1837 George Stephenson proposed a Caledonian, West Cumberland & Furness Railway, and this fanciful plan involved bridging the Duddon estuary and Morecambe Bay at an estimated combined cost of about £440,000, a huge amount of money at the time. Unsurprisingly, nothing came of this scheme but the idea stimulated the interest in railways of the Earl of Burlington (later 7th Duke of Devonshire) and the Duke of Buccleuch, both of whom had considerable land and financial interests in the Furness district. The former owned Burlington Slate Quarries on the fells above the Duddon estuary, near Kirkby-in-Furness, and soon realised the advantage of a line linking his quarries with Piel pier at Barrow-in-Furness. The Furness Railway Act (FR) for a line connecting Barrow (Piel pier) with Kirkby, and also Dalton-in-Furness, received the Royal Assent in May 1844 and it opened in August 1846; ironically slate for Ireland, rather than iron ore which later brought the area prosperity, was the first cargo. This development had not gone unnoticed by the Earl of Lonsdale, who owned coal mines around Whitehaven, and he was also keen to develop rail transport, proposing a line to link Whitehaven and Broughton-in-Furness. The Whitehaven & Furness Junction Railway (W&FJR) was incorporated in 1847 while, in the meantime, the FR extended its line from Kirkby-in-Furness to Broughton which it opened in 1848; two years later the W&FJR reached the same point. A direct line avoiding Broughton was brought into use in 1858. An extension of the FR eastwards towards Ulverston was desirable, however the townsfolk were initially hostile but later moderated their opposition. Work commenced in 1851 but was delayed by heavy earthworks with the result that Ulverston was not reached until 1854. The Ulverston & Lancaster Railway, incorporated in 1851, also had very considerable obstacles to overcome, the bridging of the Leven and Kent estuaries, and six years had elapsed before Carnforth was reached. George Stephenson's expensive and rather unrealistic plan for a line across the estuaries also stimulated interest in railways in the Maryport district and on 12th July 1837 the Maryport & Carlisle Railway was incorporated by an Act of Parliament. This 28 miles-long line was opened in stages over a period of five years, the first being purely a mineral line from Maryport to a nearby colliery that opened on 15th July 1840; the final section was completed on 10th February 1845. A southwards extension to bridge the gap between Maryport and Whitehaven was being pursued while the Carlisle line was still under construction and on 4th July 1844 the Whitehaven & Maryport Railway obtained an Act of Parliament. In the Harrington and Parton areas the line would have to be built on a ledge below geologically unstable cliffs, so the directors opted to focus initially on the Maryport to Workington stretch and this opened on 19th January 1846. The final, and most troublesome, section through Harrington to Whitehaven opened on 19th March 1847 despite the landslips that plagued construction. The line terminated at Bransty station on the northern side of Whitehaven but in 1852 a 1,333 yards-long single track tunnel was brought into use, thus enabling trains to run through to Corkickle where connection was made with the W&FJR. Photographed in particularly wintry conditions in January 1966, Stanier Class 5MT 4-6-0 No.44829, hauling the Workington portion of the 6.30am from London Euston, accelerates away from its Carnforth station stop. The equivalent train in the winter 1964/65 timetable was booked to stop at relatively minor stations such as Atherstone and Rugeley in the Trent Valley and after Carnforth it became slower still, calling at all stations to Barrow-in-Furness. This train's amazingly slack schedule continued after Barrow, from where it was advertised to leave at 3.05pm, and it dawdled along the Cumberland coast, eventually arriving at Workington (Main) at 4.51pm on Mondays to Fridays. On Saturdays the service terminated at Whitehaven where passengers for Workington were obliged to change – the final insult one might say! *Noel Machell*

A B1 class locomotive in 'foreign' territory. On 21st May 1963 Thompson B1 Class 4-6-0 No.61026 *Ourebi* powered an excursion from Lincoln to the Lake District, travelling outwards via Leeds, Skipton, Carnforth and Ulverston to Lake Side. The participants were treated to a cruise on Lake Windermere on a BR boat while their train's empty stock was moved from Lake Side to Windermere via Arnside and Hincaster Junction, on the West Coast Main Line. After the excursionists had rejoined the train later in the day it was hauled by Class 5MT No.44874 from Windermere to Arnside where the B1 Class engine was waiting to take over. The train is depicted here pulling away from Silverdale in the evening sunshine. Note that the formation appears to include a refreshment vehicle in the middle of the train. *Derrick Codling*

*CARNFORTH–BARROW–CARLISLE*

The end is nigh – well, almost. The 12.50pm Ulverston to Carnforth goods working, with BR Standard Class 4MT No.75048 in charge, rattles through Grange-over-Sands on 19th July 1968, just a few weeks before the end of BR steam on the main line system. Note the holiday-makers waving from the camping coaches on the right of the photograph. These vehicles could be found at many holiday locations throughout Great Britain, especially in the West Country, while in the Lake District sites included Hest Bank, Lake Side, Ravenglass and Seascale. These coaches were clearly not designed for the sophisticated holiday-maker and offered basic, no-frills accommodation, being doubtless promoted with a hardier clientele in mind. Camping coaches were certainly cheap, though it was often a condition that users should use rail travel to reach their accommodation. In addition to the cream and green colours depicted here, some coaches were painted in maroon while others sported Pullman livery, though the author suspects they did not offer more luxurious accommodation. *Gerald Dixon*

An unidentified northbound train pulls away from its station stop at Ravenglass on 23rd July 1958; motive power is provided by Class 2P 4-4-0 No.40654, of Barrow shed, and a Class 4MT 2-6-4T. Judging by the non-corridor stock in the train's formation this appears to have been a purely local service. Ravenglass is, of course, famous as the headquarters of the narrow gauge Ravenglass & Eskdale Railway and at the time of this photograph there were exchange sidings located on the right of the shot. *Peter Robinson*

The quiet, little seaside town of Seascale provides a delightful backdrop to this illustration of BR Standard Class 9F 2-10-0 No.92077 running through the station with a long, northbound train of empty hopper wagons on 28th July 1967. Note the small shopping parade; there can be no doubt that the station was centrally located! Seascale is an ideal choice for those seeking a restful holiday and part of a camping coach is just visible beyond the station building. The line is very close to the sea at this point and the down platform affords direct access to the shore, while between Seascale and Sellafield the railway forms the boundary between the local golf course and the sea. *Cumbrian Railways Association*

The rush hour at Sellafield. The shift pattern at the adjacent nuclear fuels processing plant determined when the rush-hour occurred at this quiet country station which would suddenly be engulfed by a mass exodus of workers at the end of each shift. In this picture, taken at the north end of the station on 20th August 1964, two workers' trains are waiting to leave while the column of smoke and steam at the other end of the station indicates that a southbound train is also awaiting departure. The precise identities of the two trains depicted is unknown but the one on the left, with Class 4F No.44065 as motive power, is believed to be bound for Moor Row while the working on the right, with Metrovick 1,200hp Co-Bo No.D5705 in charge, is possibly destined for Workington. Those diesels were not a glittering success and Barrow shed had the dubious privilege of maintaining them until they were withdrawn in the late 1960s. The station at Sellafield is very close to the sea shore but, mercifully, several feet above sea level. In times gone by Sellafield was a junction station and the line from Whitehaven (Mire House Junction) via Moor Row and Egremont converged with the former Furness Railway coastal route just north of Sellafield station. The first section was opened by the Whitehaven, Cleator & Egremont Railway on 1st July 1857 and the extension to Sellafield was brought into use on 2nd August 1869. This little-known route had an eventful history, closing as long ago as 7th January 1935 but, remarkably, it was partially reopened for workmen's services just after the end of the Second World War and was later used by school trains between Egremont and Sellafield. The former were withdrawn in September 1965 but the schools trains are believed to have continued until 3rd March 1969. *The late Derek Cross*

Between Sellafield and St Bees the line consists of a single track that runs along the seashore until the small station of St Bees is reached. St Bees is as pretty a station as one would wish to see and, moreover, is surrounded by moorland, some of which rises to a height of nearly 500 feet above sea level. This picture, which dates from the 1950s, appears to show the station looking its best following a visit from the local painting team; note the pristine paintwork of the waiting shelter at the far end of the platform, stepladders in the foreground and gas lamp standard protected by strips of wood. The distinctive signal box located at the far end of the platform is, unfortunately, hidden by the waiting shelter. Rather strangely, there is a coach berthed in a siding on the up side on the extreme right of the photograph; it may have been used by the painters but is more likely to have been a camping coach because, after all, St Bees was an absolutely ideal location far from the madding crowd. *Cumbrian Railways Association*

A young lad waits at the level crossing gates as an unidentified Stanier Class 5MT heads northwards towards Whitehaven with a goods train in tow. There is a stretch of 1 in 52 gradient between St Bees and Corkickle so, depending on the load of the train, the fireman will have some work to do. *Cumbrian Railways Association*

The attractive rural setting of St Bees is clear from this illustration of Fowler Class 4MT 2-6-4T No.42401 running into the station with an unidentified up local passenger working some time in the 1950s. Note the tiny goods yard on the left of the shot. Judging by the neat vegetable plots by the side of the line the railway authorities were keen to foster horticultural interests during this period. No.42401 was allocated to Barrow-in-Furness shed during the 1950s so it is logical to assume that Barrow was the train's destination. *Cumbrian Railways Association*

| 2069 | 2nd-SINGLE | SINGLE-2nd | 2069 |
| | Whitehaven (Bransty) to | | |
| | Whitehaven (Bransty) St. Bees | Whitehaven (Bransty) St. Bees | |
| | **ST. BEES** | | |
| | (M) 1/3 | Fare 1/3 (M) | |
| | For conditions see over | For conditions see over | |

The 5.45pm Workington to Whitehaven empty post office train, headed by Stanier 'Black Five' No.45236, winds its way slowly along the coast near Harrington station on 13th September 1967; note the severe 20mph speed restriction around the tight curve. The TPO vehicle is sandwiched between two full brake vans, the leading one being of LMSR origin while the rear van is a BR Standard design. On arrival at Whitehaven Bransty this working formed the 6.45pm SX 'Postal' to Barrow-in-Furness and called at various stations along the Cumbrian coast line. When the train arrived at Barrow it was attached to the 8.30pm SX parcels working to Preston and later continued to Huddersfield via Manchester (Victoria). It returned northwards formed in the 1.05am Huddersfield to Preston and then on to Whitehaven via Barrow. Note the banner repeater signal on the left hand side of the photograph. These are installed at locations where a signal cannot be easily sighted by train crews, such as on a very sharply curved stretch of track as seen here, and give advance warning of that signal's indication. *R. Goad/Cumbrian Railways Association*

The colliery, huge heap of pit waste and smoking chimneys in the background of this shot provide ample testament to the importance of coal and iron to the west Cumberland economy in times past. This picture was taken at Derwent Junction where a short goods branch to Merchants Quay diverges to the left behind the photographer; the colliery just visible in the distance was located at Siddick Junction where a line to Distington and Rowrah diverged from the main Carlisle to Workington route. Class 4F 0-6-0 No.44346 was photographed approaching Derwent Junction on a sunny August day in 1963. *The late Derek Cross*

Due to its geographical location Carlisle United Football Club probably spends a higher proportion of its income on transport costs that any other team in the English league, the only other team in near proximity having been Workington Town. On Boxing Day 1963 the teams met in a Derby match and BR obligingly laid on a special to convey Carlisle supporters to and from the game. No expense was spared, BR really entering into the spirit of the occasion by turning out one of Upperby shed's dwindling band of 'Royal Scot' Class 4-6-0s to work the train. Here, No.46141 *The North Staffordshire Regiment* is depicted on the outward journey just beyond Dalston station. One wonders how many locomotives of this class ever ventured along the old Maryport and Carlisle line. On the same day four years later Carlisle United played Blackpool for which BR Standard Pacific No.70013 *Oliver Cromwell,* in sparkling external condition, was rostered to take fans to and from the match. This proved to be a very historic occasion because these trains were the last BR steam passenger workings over Shap summit; on the return run the crew stopped for water at Tebay and the fireman went to the shed to request banking assistance. Alas, the shed was in darkness and the staff were doubtless still enjoying their Christmas break; there were no locomotives in steam so No.70013 made the ascent of Shap from a standing start in Tebay station giving a memorable display of the raw power of steam traction. *Bob Leslie/Peter Robinson collection*

In the middle of the 19th century the iron industry in west Cumberland was developing rapidly and there was a growing need for coke for the area's furnaces, and the local ironmasters were aware that a cross-Pennine route from County Durham to Penrith was planned. The coke available locally had a high phosphoric content and was therefore unsuitable for use in iron production, and thoughts turned to the idea of a line to link with that route and enable high quality coke from County Durham to reach west Cumberland's furnaces. In December 1860 a bill for the construction of the Cockermouth Keswick and Penrith Railway (CKPR) was deposited in Parliament; the bill was passed and received the Royal Assent on 1st August 1861. An end-on connection with the London and North Western Railway was made at Cockermouth, thus giving access to industrial west Cumberland. Goods workings along the line commenced on 4th November 1864 while passenger trains started running on 2nd January 1865. A particularly interesting, and little-known, feature of the line was the spur just south of Penrith from Eamont Bridge Junction to Redhills Junction on the CKPR; this enabled mineral trains to run directly from the Kirkby Stephen to Penrith Eden Valley line to the CKPR without the need to reverse in Penrith station. The iron industry in west Cumberland became self-sufficient for coke after the First World War and cross-Pennine traffic declined with the result that the spur became moribund and was closed on 5th June 1937. The loss of goods traffic on the Penrith to Workington line was serious enough but in the 1920s passenger traffic started to ebb away due to competition from motor buses and, even worse, the advent of private motoring after the end of the Second World War. The section west of Keswick was closed in April 1966, the truncated line eastwards to Penrith surviving for a further six years until the inevitable came on 6th March 1972. In this portrait Ivatt Class 2MT 2-6-0 No.46432 is seen making a smoky exit from Penrith with a train bound for Workington on 29th June 1965. *Bob Leslie/Peter Robinson collection*

Stanier Class 5MT 4-6-0 No.45197 exerts maximum effort as it gets to grips with the steep climb away from the West Coast Main Line; the town of Penrith can be discerned in the background. The train is the 10.00am Newcastle-upon-Tyne to Keswick which was quite a heavy load by the modest standards of this line and the shot was taken on 5th August 1956. This train was routed via Carlisle, where it reversed, and arrived at Keswick at 1.06pm. Note the goods train in the loop on the right of the picture. *Bob Leslie/Peter Robinson collection*

A really evocative scene at Redhills, just west of the point where the Keswick line converges with the West Coast Main Line, showing Ivatt Class 2MT 2-6-0 46458 heading westwards on 3rd July 1965. The photographer seems to have had luck with the sun, which is shining defiantly despite the substantial cloud cover and, for a change, the locomotive is in quite clean condition. The smoke effect is also helping to create a very attractive image! *Bob Leslie/Peter Robinson collection*

The Stephenson Locomotive Society/Manchester Locomotive Society 'Lakes & Fells' rail tour is depicted at Flusco, west of Blencow, on 2nd April 1966. Despite the fact that a blizzard had been forecast throughout the north-west of England, incredibly it was agreed that the special would run as scheduled. Stanier 'Jubilee' Class 6P5F No.45596 *Bahamas* hauled the train from Manchester (Exchange) as far as Hellifield where the legendary Gresley Class A3 Pacific No.4472 *Flying Scotsman* took over but it was already running almost an hour late due to snow clearance on the line north of Blackburn. No.4472 worked the train over the Settle & Carlisle line and then down to Penrith on the West Coast Main Line. A journey over the line to Workington then ensued with motive power being provided by Ivatt Class 2MT 2-6-0s Nos.46458 and 46426, both of which were in sparkling condition. This train was the last steam-hauled passenger train to traverse the entire Penrith to Workington route; note that despite the bitterly cold conditions some especially enthusiastic participants are leaning out of carriage windows. Later the train continued along the Cumberland coast to Arnside where arrival was over two hours late and some participants were clearly worried about getting home safely, and returned to Preston by diesel train. Despite the dreadful weather the rail tour proceeded to Hellifield as booked, with *Flying Scotsman* again in charge for the short run from Arnside, and at Hellifield *Bahamas* took over once again for the journey to Manchester where it arrived at just after midnight on the Sunday morning. Fifteen inches of snow had apparently fallen in Manchester during the day so it must have been quite a challenge trying to get home by public transport at that time on a Sunday morning. Quite a day to remember!
*Bob Leslie/Peter Robinson collection*

2nd-SINGLE    SINGLE-2nd
2989          Penrith to          2989
Penrith                      Penrith
Blencow        **BLENCOW**       Blencow
(M)    1/0    Fare    1/0    (M)
For conditions see over   For conditions see over

Super power on the Keswick line! The 10.00am SuO Newcastle-upon-Tyne to Keswick is seen again, this time near Flusco with the local quarry in the background. Motive power on this occasion is Stanier 'Royal Scot' Class 7P 4-6-0 No.46141 *The North Staffordshire Regiment* and this portrait was taken on 11th August 1957. This dated train conveyed a restaurant car and in the 1959 timetable ran from 15th June until 6th September.
*Bob Leslie/Peter Robinson collection*

Photographed against a splendid backdrop of towering Lake District mountains, Ivatt Class 2MT 2-6-0 No.46432 is seen again, this time heading westwards near Troutbeck with a Penrith train on 1st July 1964. In the 1964/65 winter timetable a modest service of six trains was advertised on weekdays only and there was also a short working between Penrith and Keswick during the middle of the day. The average journey time between Penrith and Workington was about 1¼ hours for the 39¾ miles between the towns; the trains called at all stations so there was ample time to admire the magnificent scenery. Note that the train's formation consisted of a composite corridor (CK) coach sandwiched between two brake composite corridor (BCK) vehicles so there was almost as much first class accommodation as second. *Rodney Lissenden*

Troutbeck, seen here looking westwards, was a classic country station situated in the middle of nowhere but at least a hostelry was next door to the station which must have provided comfort to many weary travellers over the years; the bridge carried the road to Patterdale and Ullswater. The station was located in a beautiful setting, and some of the Lake District's most majestic peaks were close by, but hidden by the trees in this photograph. The staff clearly took immense pride in their station which was immaculately kept. In the late 19th century operation of the line between Threlkeld and Troutbeck was bedevilled by the stiff gradients between the two stations, consisting of stretches of 1 in 68 and 1 in 62, and these slowed trains thus reducing line capacity. This section was doubled in the mid-1890s to alleviate the problem. This portrait of Troutbeck station was taken on 1st July 1964. *Rodney Lissenden*

The Penrith to Workington line, which passed through the heart of the Lake District, was undoubtedly one of the most spectacular in Great Britain as exemplified here by this stunning shot of the London-bound 'Lakes Express' on the double track section between Threlkeld and Troutbeck. The locomotives are a pair of Ivatt Class 2MTs, Nos.46455 and 46491, and this portrait was taken on 15th August 1959. This was the main train of the day on the route and on Mondays to Fridays left Workington at 8.55am, and stopped at most stations to Penrith where it reversed. Surprisingly perhaps, it stopped at Tebay on its way to London and was combined with a portion from Windermere at Oxenholme from where it was advertised to depart at 11.50am, almost three hours after leaving Workington! The advertised arrival time at London Euston was 5.40pm. The Windermere portion even conveyed a restaurant car – those were the days! *Bob Leslie/Peter Robinson collection*

Keswick was the most important intermediate traffic centre on the Penrith to Workington line and in this shot tender-first Ivatt Class 2MT 2-6-0 No.46491 is depicted taking water at the west end of the station some time in the 1960s. Note the substantially constructed water tank and elegant platform canopies. Keswick station was well equipped to deal with passenger traffic and had three platforms, carriage sidings and a turntable. The goods yard, located west of the station on the down side of the line, comprised six sidings and there was a goods shed plus facilities for dealing with coal traffic and cattle. The closure of the line was a protracted affair over a period of six years and when the section west of here was shut in 1966 Keswick station became the end of the line. The track was reduced to the bare minimum and the once bustling station looked very sad and neglected and, perhaps, it came as a relief when the line was finally put out of its misery, closing, as previously stated, from 6th March 1972.
*RCTS Photo Archive*

The tiny station of Braithwaite was located in a glorious setting, surrounded by mountains, just over two miles from Keswick and close to Bassenthwaite Lake and Derwent Water. Note the cream and green camping coach in the goods yard: the railway authorities always chose the most idyllic locations for their camping coaches and Braithwaite must have been among the best. This was a particularly attractive location because the station was in a quiet position at the end of a drive off the main road, yet very close to the village. A small group of people appear to be playing in the goods yard; perhaps they were resident in the camping coach when this picture was taken on sunny 24th August 1963. *Roy Denison*

A comprehensive view of the layout at Cockermouth showing the signal box, track layout and goods yard with its cattle pens on the extreme right; the station was located south of the town centre. The yard seems to have been reasonably busy at the time of this picture. In times gone by there was a turntable at the far end of the station layout, on the left hand side. A relic that survived here was the goods shed, situated some way to the west of the station, which was formerly the engine shed for the erstwhile Cockermouth and Workington Railway. *Roy Denison*

After traversing the breathtaking Lakeland mountains the line from Penrith terminated at the industrial coastal town of Workington where connection was made with trains on the Carlisle to Barrow-in-Furness line. In this picture Fairburn Class 4MT 2-6-4T No.42119 poses in Workington (Main) station with an unidentified passenger working on 24th August 1963; at the time of this photograph No.42119 was allocated to Barrow shed so it was presumably working a service along the Cumbrian coast. There were originally two other stations in Workington, Bridge station on the Cockermouth & Workington Railway, which closed from 1st January 1951, and Central station on the Cleator & Workington Junction Railway from which passenger trains were withdrawn on 13th April 1931. In bygone days the number of stations in the town caused confusion among the townsfolk which was resolved to some degree when the principal Workington station was given the suffix 'Main' by the LMSR after the grouping.
*Roy Denison*

During an idle moment, a member of Foxfield station's staff poses with a platform barrow on a sunny day some time in the 1950s. The station is delightfully situated at the head of the Duddon estuary but it is unlikely a station would have been built on this spot if George Stephenson's ambitious plan to cross the estuary had come to fruition. The station was an architectural curiosity and a joy for any railway historian and still retains a little of its character even today. On the left of the picture the solid, stone-built goods shed is partially visible while also in view on the left is the small train shed, also built no doubt using local stone. But while the former has an arched entrance, in contrast the train shed's arch appears to have been modified at some stage and most

of it replaced. In the foreground are an ornate platform seat, oil lamp and a small rockery which all add to the station's undoubted charm. Needless to say the station nameboard is of the old 'hawkseye' design. The principal part of the station building in view appears to be the gentlemen's toilet while beyond it can be seen the roof of the signal box. The branch trains to Coniston started from the southbound platform – note the starting signal. Latterly, these were generally formed of a 'pull-push' set so the locomotive did not have to run-round its train, a most convenient arrangement. The fells beyond the station are on the southernmost fringe of the Lake District. *Cumbrian Railways Association*

Two smartly attired members of BR staff stroll along the platform at Foxfield apparently oblivious to the arrival of Stanier Class 5MT No.45230 which seems to have come from the Coniston branch. The gentleman on the right appears to be the station master who, perhaps, lived in the house on the right of the picture. The booking office window and station clock can just be discerned between the stanchions on the left. The 9½ miles-long line to Coniston was incorporated on 10th August 1857, the branch opening to passenger traffic on 18th June 1859, and to goods trains the following year when an extension to the copper mines was brought into use. The Coniston branch was probably the most remote and inaccessible from the main centres of population of all the Lake District branch lines so it is perhaps not surprising it was closed to passenger traffic from 6th October 1958 and completely from 30th April 1962.
*Cumbrian Railways Association*

A joint Stephenson Locomotive Society/Manchester Locomotive Society rail tour visited Coniston station, which was still open for goods traffic at this time, on 27th August 1961 and participants are seen here having a look round the premises while Class 4F No.44347 simmers on one of the platform roads. Most probably realised that this would be the last occasion they would be able to reach Coniston by train and, indeed, the line was closed completely, as previously mentioned, the following April. The tracks continued some distance beyond the station to the mines. The early railway companies were quick to exploit the tourist potential of Coniston Water and introduced steamer services, even though the pier was some distance from the station, but this traffic was seasonal and doubtless all-year-round passenger traffic was meagre. *Edwin Wilmshurst*

Coniston station was beautifully situated as seen in this shot; the date of the picture is unknown but it seems to have been taken in the 1950s before the withdrawal of passenger services; certainly everything is spick and span. The engine shed was a sub-shed of Barrow and presumably closed when the passenger trains ceased to run. *Stuart Ackley collection*

Stanier 'Jubilee' Class 6P5F No.45696 *Arethusa* is seen near Newby Bridge with the 11.00am Preston to Lake Side train on 2nd June 1962. There was a considerable amount of tender-first running due to the need for trains to reverse at Ulverston to gain access to the branch. Like neighbouring Haverthwaite, Newby Bridge station has an interesting history for such a small, obscure station. It was 'temporarily' closed from 12th September 1939, on the outbreak of the Second World War, and the railway authorities clearly thought its prospects of attracting traffic were negligible, particularly bearing in mind its location across the river from Newby Bridge which was little more than a hamlet consisting of a few cottages. The station's closure was made permanent from 12th July 1949. When the preservationists moved in the vegetation that had become established on Newby Bridge's platform was cleared and the tiny halt is now very much back on the map despite 30 years of total abandonment. *Noel Machell*

Haverthwaite station, virtually surrounded by dense woodland, is now the southern terminus of the preserved section of the Lake Side branch. In this view Stanier Class 5MT 4-6-0 No.45386 is seen running into the station with a train to Ulverston in the early 1960s. Haverthwaite station has a curious history and was officially closed from 16th September 1940 for the duration of the Second World War. It reopened again from 3rd June 1946 and had an advertised passenger service until 29th September 1946 when it closed for the winter. The station did not reopen for the 1947 summer season, however, but was not officially closed until 13th June 1955. The rail connection to Backbarrow foundries, for so long one of the line's major customers, was a long siding reached from Haverthwaite goods yard. The line from Ulverston along the estuary of the river Leven to Newby Bridge was proposed by the Furness Railway (FR), the first sod being cut by James Ramsden, General Manager of the FR, at Haverthwaite on 22nd November 1866. The company soon realised that an extension to the shores of Lake Windermere would be commercially desirable and the line opened throughout to Lake Side station on 1st June 1869. The FR constructed a quay at Lake Side to facilitate transfer between the trains and steamers. The coming of the railways enabled the masses to take day trips for the first time and a substantial proportion of the passenger traffic comprised people simply taking a boat trip on the lake as part of a day out, rather than local travellers. There was also substantial goods

traffic, including coal for the lake steamers and iron ore for Backbarrow iron works. The FR bought the lake steamers in 1872 and the line enjoyed a wonderful period of prosperity prior to the First World War. The line's heyday was undoubtedly during this period before road transport became more commonplace and a slow decline started, culminating in 1938 in the withdrawal of passenger trains during the winter months; the summer service also was withdrawn during the Second World War. After the end of the war much of the line's holiday traffic was undermined by the increase in coach travel and private motoring, and BR proposed closure of the line to passengers. This was implemented from 6th September 1965, part of the branch remaining open for goods traffic but this ceased in April 1967, the last train under BR jurisdiction being a brake van special run for enthusiasts in September 1967. The section between Lake Side and Haverthwaite, as previously stated, is now preserved but, alas, the rest of the line fell victim to the inevitable road improvement scheme and the opportunity to save the entire branch was lost. *The late Derek Cross*

The branch terminated at Lake Side station on the southern tip of Lake Windermere, and is probably one of the most pleasantly situated stations in Great Britain; it is in a tranquil position away from a main road and surrounded by trees. When this picture was taken on 28th August 1964 some track had been lifted in the goods yard but otherwise the station and its environs were largely intact and today the site is still in use by the Lakeside and Haverthwaite Railway. Note the camping coach and ornate water tank on the left of the shot; an engineman sits in the foreground by the former cattle dock while his locomotive takes water. In the background the station's short overall roof can be seen while on the right is the quay from where boats plied up Lake Windermere to Bowness-on-Windermere and Ambleside. Could one wish for a more enchanting journey?
*Gavin Morrison*

The Furness Railway was responsible for some outstanding station designs, Ulverston being one of its principal architectural gems, but the station building at Lake Side was also outstanding. The station frontage is depicted in this shot, which was apparently taken from a boat, on 22nd July 1963. Tragically, the station was demolished in stages between 1965 and 1973 following the closure of the branch; the roof and its supports were the last structures to be torn down, in 1978, apparently because they had been declared unsafe. If the building had survived it would undoubtedly be one of the most impressive preserved stations in Great Britain. Surely, a tragic loss? *Rodney Lissenden*

Steam to the rescue! BR's fleet of diesel multiple units was not known for its reliability and in this picture a failed Derby Lightweight 2-car unit is seen ignominiously being towed back to a maintenance depot for repair. The locomotive hauling the disgraced unit is Stanier Class 5MT No.44877 and this portrait was taken just over a mile south of Staveley on a sunny 10th June 1968. Construction of the 10 miles-long branch from Oxenholme to Birthwaite (which later developed into the town of Windermere) was authorised on 30th June 1845 and the first stretch as far as Kendal opened for traffic on 22nd September 1846. The building of the line was vehemently opposed by William Wordsworth who thought the scheme would desecrate his beloved Lakeland landscape but, nonetheless, Windermere was reached and the line fully opened on 20th April 1847. *Tommy Tomalin*

An Oxenholme to Windermere local train is depicted near Ings, between Staveley and Windermere, in May 1965. Motive power is provided by Fowler Class 4MT 2-6-4T No.42322 which is running bunker first. Constructed at Derby works and released to traffic in May 1928, No.42322 was withdrawn from service just two months after this shot was taken; a total of 125 of these machines was built but only 14 survived into 1965, so No.42322 was one of the last operational examples. *Roy Hobbs*

Judging by the number of people standing around in Windermere goods yard the visit of 'Black Five' No.44894 on the daily goods working seems to be a major talking point. This is explained by the fact that the picture was taken on 1st August 1968 during the final week of standard gauge steam operation on BR, and for some of those present this may have been the last time they would see a steam engine in normal traffic at Windermere so it really was quite an occasion. The *very* last steam working to Windermere is thought to have been on 2nd August when No.44709 powered the daily goods and returned to Carnforth with various chalked inscriptions on its smokebox door. Surprisingly, Windermere was not the northern limit of steam operation during the last few weeks of steam traction because there were sporadic workings as far north as Tebay and Shap with ballast trains. *Roy Hobbs*

Those were the days at Windermere, when the station boasted no fewer than four platforms, an overall roof and a commodious goods yard. When this picture was taken on 6th June 1968 there was even steam traction to enliven the place, the locomotive seen here being Stanier Class 5MT 4-6-0 No.45025. The locomotive is coupled to a LMSR-designed carriage and brake van and one can only assume that the coach had suffered a brake defect that could not be rectified on the spot by a fitter and was being taken away for attention. Very sadly, the station and its environs were later subjected to over-zealous 'rationalisation' and the attractive station building suffered the ultimate indignity, being converted into a supermarket. A soulless, new station with vastly reduced facilities was brought into use in 1986. The summer 1963 timetable lists a number of trains to London, including the 'Lakes Express', and direct services on Saturdays to Leeds and Liverpool. A particularly interesting working was the 8.30pm from Windermere to London which also conveyed portions from Workington and Blackpool; this train ran up the West Coast Main Line as far as Crewe and then was not shown in the public timetables, apart from an entry quoting an arrival time of 3.35am at St Pancras! *Tommy Tomalin*